English Mystery

The Red Fog

Woods Delaney

Compact Verlag

Bisher sind in dieser Reihe erschienen:
- Englisch: B1, B2

In der Reihe Compact Lernkrimi sind erschienen:
- Englisch, Französisch, Italienisch, Spanisch: B1, B2
- Englisch GB/US, Business English: B1, B2
- Deutsch: B1
- Sammelband Lernkrimi Englisch: B1/B2

In der Reihe Compact Lernkrimi Kurzkrimis sind erschienen:
- Englisch, Französisch, Italienisch, Spanisch, Deutsch: A2

In der Reihe Compact Lernkrimi History sind erschienen:
- Englisch: B1, B2, Italienisch: B1

In der Reihe Compact Lernthriller sind erschienen:
- Englisch: B1, B2
- Spanisch: B1

In der Reihe Compact Lernkrimi Hörbuch sind erschienen:
- Englisch: B1, B2, Business English: B2
- Französisch, Italienisch, Spanisch: B1

In der Reihe Compact Lernkrimi Sprachkurs sind erschienen:
- Englisch für Anfänger: A1/A2

Lernziele:
- Grundwortschatz, Grammatik (A2, B1)
- Aufbauwortschatz, Konversation (B2)

In der Reihe Compact Schüler-Lernkrimi sind erschienen:
- Englisch, Französisch, Spanisch, Latein, Deutsch, Mathematik, Physik, Chemie

Weitere Titel sind in Vorbereitung.

Chefredaktion: Dr. Angela Sendlinger
Redaktion: Gesa Füßle
Fachredaktion: Fiona Cain
Produktion: Wolfram Friedrich
Titelillustration: Karl Knospe
Typographischer Entwurf: Maria Seidel
Umschlaggestaltung: Carsten Abelbeck

ISBN-13: 978-3-8174-7574-2
7275746

Besuchen Sie uns im Internet: www.compactverlag.de, www.lernkrimi.de

Vorwort

Mit der neuen, spannenden Compact Lernstory Mystery können Sie Ihre Englischkenntnisse auf schnelle und einfache Weise vertiefen, auffrischen und überprüfen.
Parapsychologin Dr. Solina Black erleichtert das Sprachtraining mit Spannung und Nervenkitzel. Sie und ihre mysteriösen Fälle stehen im Mittelpunkt einer zusammenhängenden Story.
Die Mystery-Story wird auf jeder Seite durch abwechslungsreiche und kurzweilige Übungen ergänzt, die das Lernen unterhaltsam und spannend machen.
Prüfen Sie Ihr Englisch in Lückentexten, Zuordnungs- und Übersetzungsaufgaben, in Buchstabenspielen und Kreuzworträtseln!
Ob im Bus oder in der Bahn, im Wartezimmer, zu Hause oder in der Mittagspause – das Sprachtraining im handlichen Format bietet die ideale Trainingsmöglichkeit für zwischendurch.
Schreiben Sie die Lösungen einfach ins Buch!
Die richtigen Antworten sind in einem eigenen Lösungsteil zusammengefasst.

Und nun kann das übersinnliche Vergnügen beginnen …

Viel Spaß und Erfolg!

Die Ereignisse und die handelnden Personen in diesem Buch sind frei erfunden. Etwaige Ähnlichkeiten mit tatsächlichen Ereignissen oder lebenden Personen wären rein zufällig und unbeabsichtigt.

Inhalt

Story

Dr. Solina Black ist Parapsychologin und lebt in Manchester. Sie, ihr Assistent Henry Wheatherly und ihr Shetland-Schäferhund scheinen merkwürdige Gegebenheiten geradezu anzuziehen. Immer, wenn Dr. Black in der Nähe ist, ereignen sich mysteriöse Fälle – und stets schafft sie es, das Geheimnis zu lüften.

Der Frühling in Manchester hat gerade begonnen und Dr. Black freut sich schon darauf, die warmen Abende im Freien zu genießen. Aber die Idylle wird zerstört, als sie eines Abends ein rotes Leuchten über der Stadt entdeckt. Wie sich bald herausstellen wird, handelt es sich um einen roten Nebel – und jedes Mal, wenn er sich nachts über die Stadt senkt, geschieht ein Verbrechen. Bringt der rote Nebel die Menschen dazu, ihre dunkle Seite zu zeigen? Oder hilft er Kriminellen, ihre Tat ungesehen zu verüben? Und warum greift die Polizei nicht ein?

Mit der Hilfe von Weatherly macht sich Dr. Black auf die Suche nach der Ursache des roten Nebels. Was steckt hinter dem Phänomen? Kann sie das Rätsel lösen und den Nebel aufhalten?

The Red Fog

It was late one evening in early spring, and Dr Solina Black was strolling back to her house, gazing up at the stars. The ten-minute walk home from her local pub was waking her up. She had just left the warmth of a pub, and the quiet conversation had made her a little sleepy. Outside, the night sky was slightly cloudy, and the air was cool. A few stars were shining brightly and a half moon was setting the high-flying clouds aglow. She was slowly making her way home, enjoying the feeling that winter was finally over. Even the stars, so far away, no longer seemed as cold as they had a month earlier. In the pub, her discussion of Carlos Castaneda's *Don Juan* books and Joseph Chilton Pearce's *Crack in the Cosmic Egg* with a psychology student had been only moderately interesting. It was always the same: once a psychology student learned that she was a parapsychologist, these two authors – and a few others – came up for discussion. Whether the soul could, for short periods of time, leave the body or not was a subject that interested her, but it was also an easy target for those who believed parapsychology to be a ridiculous field of study. This evening's discussion at the pub had been nothing new at all, though the student had not made her position on the subject clear. Dr Black didn't mind serving as a representative for parapsychology, but she wished that the students who wanted to challenge it would come up with new arguments.

ÜBUNG 1 !

Übung 1: Bilden Sie aus dem Adjektiv ein Substantiv!

1. warm warmth
2. sleepy sleep
3. bright brightness

4. cold	cold
5. interesting	interest
6. beautiful	beauty

She stopped and stood up straight. It was not fear that someone was following her that made her stop. It was not the sky directly overhead that caught her attention. There was no loud sound, nor were there any whispered words. She took off her small, round glasses, pulled out a piece of silk and cleaned them. Putting them back on, the night was clearer and she turned her gaze to the north. There was, unmistakably, a red glow on the horizon. The horizon wasn't distant, however; this red glow was somewhere over Manchester, not far away at all. There was no orange in the glow, so – for better or for worse – it was not a fire. In fact, looking a little closer at it, she thought, "That isn't just red, that's blood-red."

! ÜBUNG 2

Übung 2: Finden Sie das passende Gegenteil! Setzen Sie die richtige Ziffer ein!

1. straight	[5] close
2. loud	[4] square
3. whisper	[1] winding
4. round	[6] dangerous
5. distant	[2] quiet
6. safe	[3] shout

"Or maybe you're just getting excited over nothing," she said to herself after a minute. "It's that second pint of stout you shouldn't have had. Your judgement is off a bit now. It is a strange glow, though. But there must be a logical explanation, so just go on about your business, Solina. Stop thinking about things that have nothing to do with you. You're just not sure what you're seeing, that's all. A couple of pints of stout and your imagination goes wild." Dr Black began walking again and arrived home without any further excitement.

Her dreams that night, unfortunately, were not without excitement. She was walking up to lots of different doors, and under each of them she noticed a spreading red glow. Many times she paused with her hand upon the doorknob. "Do you want to know what is on the other side? Do you really want to know?" That question kept repeating itself and, along with it, the question of whether she could get outside herself, because if she could not, then she, Solina Black, parapsychologist, could not escape the red glow. Naturally, in order to get out, she was forced to answer the question: "Where am I?"

There was a newspaper in the room on the other side of the door. If she would only turn the doorknob and walk in, it would be there waiting for her. It was a newspaper that could explain everything.

Übung 3: Setzen Sie die Wörter an den richtigen Stellen ein!
(prepare, woke, restfulness, mind-reader, clients, bottom, busy, advertisement)

ÜBUNG 3 !

She 1. ____________ in the morning feeling very tired. A 2. ____________ night of dreaming had robbed her sleep of its 3. ________ ____. "No 4. ____________ until this afternoon," she thought, "but I have to 5. ____________ for them."

She opened the newspaper to the local section and, there on the fourth page, found her 6. ______________, in the centre of which was her picture. "For a picture in the newspaper," she said to herself, "it's okay. I don't look half-dead, in any case." Dr Solina Black, with her degrees, her specialities, and then, at the 7. ______________, a disclaimer and a promise: "I am not a 8. ______________, but if others have been unable to help you then I can." Like a solicitor, Dr Black fully expected to get her share of eccentrics ringing up, but maybe some of them would be interesting and maybe some of them really *could* use her help.

Dr Black had been back in Manchester for only a month. She had gone to the University of Manchester between the ages of 19 and 22 and then to the University of London where she met and worked with her mentor, Dr Eileen Grimes. After gaining her doctorate in parapsychology, she had worked with Dr Grimes for two years. "I'm a mother bird throwing you out of the nest," Dr Grimes had told her. "It's time you flew on your own. Stay here in London or go to the north of Scotland, it doesn't matter, but you have to work on your own." There had been no tears as the brief though successful partnership was terminated. Neither woman was particularly sentimental.

ÜBUNG 4 !

Übung 4: Unterstreichen Sie die richtige Übersetzung!

1. judgement	Unheil/Urteil
2. glow	glühen/brennen

3. gaze — erstarren/starren
4. spread — verschweigen/verbreiten
5. disclaimer — Gegenerklärung/Gegner

But if Dr Solina Black had a weakness, it was for her Shetland sheepdog, Eugene. When she wasn't working, he was the focus of her attention. She had had Eugene since he was an eight-week-old puppy.
If dogs can form even slightly complex thoughts, then there must have been times when Eugene thought to himself, “Of all the people in the world, I had to meet up with a parapsychologist who is absolutely passionate about what she does.” When Eugene got scared on a walk because something strange happened, he stopped and sat down right in the middle of the pavement. This dog is stopping here, his eyes said. Unfortunately for Eugene, strange things often happened when Dr Black was around. There seemed to be no cure for it. She was a magnet for strange occurrences, and Eugene had to share her with them.

Übung 5: Übersetzen Sie!

1. Dr Black hatte eine Schwäche für ihren Hund Eugene.

____

____

2. Sie bekam Eugene, als er ein Welpe war.

____

3. Eugenes Gedanken waren sehr komplex.

____

4. Eugene hatte auf Spaziergängen oft Angst und setzte sich auf den Bürgersteig.

---

5. Eugene musste seine Besitzerin mit merkwürdigen Erscheinungen teilen.

So, Dr Black had at last returned to Manchester. She had loved the city as a student and now hoped that she would feel at home again in it as a professional. A native of Swindon, she couldn't see herself returning to her hometown. Strange little Solina Black who always seemed to be in trouble, such was her reputation in the town of her birth. In Manchester, she was no one, except to some of her professors at University who welcomed her return. In the month since she had moved into a large house in Didsbury with a servant's quarters at the back, she had received a good many of her professors' students. She had even considered renting out the servant's quarters to one or two students, but then she decided not to since she would rather have peace and quiet than a little extra money each month.

ÜBUNG 6 !

Übung 6: Bringen Sie die Wörter in die richtige Reihenfolge!

1. of studied Dr had University the Black at Manchester

---

2. her the in University psychology finished at she of studies London

3. Black passionate she Dr about what always did very was

4. decided to Dr had Manchester return Black to

Through her advertisement, then, she hoped to get some work that would offer a challenge and would, quite naturally, also help pay the bills.

When people experienced things that could not be explained but were of no interest to the police, they came to Dr Black. When something was wrong but no one else believed it or understood it, people came to her for help. When nothing was wrong and nothing was right, people came to Dr Solina Black because something strange was going on and she could be trusted to get to the bottom of it.

ÜBUNG 7 !

Übung 7: Beantworten Sie die Fragen zum Text!

1. What colour was the fog Dr Black saw over Manchester?

2. What did Dr Black find in the newspaper the next morning?

3. For how long had Dr Black been back in Manchester again?

4. When did she study at the University of Manchester?

5. Who was Dr Eileen Grimes?

6. Where was Dr Black born?

Two nights later she saw the red glow again in the sky high over Manchester. "That isn't normal. Something is afoot; something is definitely happening. I should have trusted myself the other night," she thought. "That's apparently one lesson I'll never learn. This time," she decided, "I'll go and see where the glow is and see if I can find out what it is and what's causing it."

She put on her helmet, started her scooter and drove into the city. She got off before the red glow was upon her and started walking towards it. Hanging low over this part of the city something was glowing red. "It looks different from Didsbury," thought Dr Black. "From here it looks more like a red fog. There's a heaviness to the glow. It's milky rather than rainwater-clear." She looked up at the red glowing fog but could not determine any source for the colour. There was no red light focused up at the fog and nothing shining down from above. "You can't just add food colouring to clouds and fog," she thought.

"There's no red dye that will turn your grey fog red, but the red has to come from somewhere." The fog seemed to be descending as Dr Black approached it. It was coming down as if it wanted to meet her. She stopped walking, but the fog continued its slow descent. "It isn't coming to meet me," she thought, starting on her way again, "but I am coming to meet it." Down it came, the red fog, slower than dry snowflakes; down it came, slower than a fully-loaded container ship entering Salford Quays. And there was motion within the fog, as if clouds were moving back and forth inside it.

Übung 8: Übersetzen Sie und enträtseln Sie das Lösungswort!

! ÜBUNG 8

1. Helm _ _ ☐ _ _ _
2. Nebel _ ☐ _
3. Motorroller _ _ ☐ _ _ _ _
4. bestimmen _ _ _ _ _ _ _ ☐ _
5. Schwere _ _ _ _ ☐ _ _ _ _
6. Lektion ☐ _ _ _ _
7. Wolken _ _ _ _ _ ☐

Lösung: _ _ _ _ _ _ _

It was not a normal fog, she noticed, as it poured into the street. There seemed to be a beginning, which moved towards her, and she thought she could see an end to it in the distance. "Now, that's no natural phenomenon," she reflected, "or none that I ever heard of." She also realised that what she had taken to be a glow was simply the colour of the fog and, perhaps, light from the moon reflecting off it. It was, in any case, not some light coming from within the fog. "It isn't an unidentified flying object," she thought, "but it isn't natural either. Unless it's a rare, natural occurrence, like a so-called blue moon."

Übung 9: Unterstreichen Sie die richtige Alternative!

She (1.) departed/arrived at a street of terraced houses over which the red fog seemed about to settle. Dr Black considered warning people. "Should I (2.) scream/sleep in the street or bang on their doors? What can I do to let them know that there's a red fog overhead? And what should I warn them (3.) about/off? I don't know that they're in any real danger, and yet I'm standing here – a safe distance away – hoping there is no danger."
Down came the red fog, down onto the houses, settling onto the street, and now a glow came from within, a glow (4.) of/from the streetlamps. There was the sound (5.) of/from water meeting electricity, a rather shocking handshake, and all the lamps in the street went (6.) on/out at once. Except (7.) of/for the fog, which seemed to contain (8.) it's/its own light, the street was now dark.

With the darkness came an absolute silence: Dr Black heard nothing. She looked in all directions, but except for the fog there was no movement anywhere. She was the only person in the street. "Eugene," she thought, "would be very unhappy if he were here, but he's sitting at home unhappy because he isn't here with me. Everything seems dead now."
From out of this stillness, a taxi quietly appeared. It stopped a short distance from the red fog and sat waiting. Dr Black stood a moment, and then began to walk towards the taxi. "What," she wanted to know, "is the taxi driver waiting for? Here, in front of the red fog, seems an unlikely place for a passenger."

Suddenly, Dr Black saw two people, a man and a woman, emerge from the fog and run towards the taxi. The man was carrying a thin briefcase and led the way. He opened the back door, helped the woman inside, and then got inside himself. The closing of the door, though muffled, was the loudest sound the street had heard for some time. There was a brief pause and then the taxi turned around and headed away from the red fog. On the side of the taxi, Dr Black read *Your Car.* "I'll have to find out who those people are and where they are going," she said to herself.
In time, the red fog began to lift and move away until it had faded from sight. Dr Black stayed until it was just about completely gone.

Übung 10: Ordnen Sie die Buchstaben zu sinnvollen Wörtern!

1. There was absolute __________ (leiccns) on the streets.

2. This __________ (lstisnels) was strange.

3. There was no light __________ (xtecep) for the red glow of the fog.

4. The __________ (eesapsrng) got out of the taxi.

5. He put the documents in his __________ (sabreicef).

6. He __________ (cetlomepyl) lost his mind.

The streetlights did not come back on, and she decided that she would come back tomorrow during the day to see if there were reports of anything strange. She was also curious about whether the lights would work again. Dr Black drove her scooter slowly through several blocks to Deansgate Road, and then she pushed the speed up to 45 miles per hour, which was about as fast as the old scooter could go, and went home. Though it was 1 am when she arrived back, she could not sleep right away. She let Eugene out in the backyard for a few minutes and then went upstairs into her study and looked through a few books, trying to find historical records about fogs, especially red fogs. Was there anything in the history books about such phenomena? She read of fogs that had brought illnesses and death, but they had not been red. It was, also, not absolutely certain the fogs had been the cause of any deaths. The writers admitted that it might only have been an unfortunate coincidence. People, already scared and upset, quite easily became hysterical when such natural phenomena occurred.

The next morning, Dr Black rang up *Your Car* and asked for the driver who had picked up the two people running out of the terraced houses late the previous night. After a brief search, the manager at *Your Car* was able to determine who the driver was. "He'll be in just before 4 pm," he told her. "He works four to midnight again tonight." She then scanned the newspaper for reports of anything strange in the sky the previous night, but she did not find any. There was also no mention of anything abnormal in the area where she had seen the fog. Nothing, she realised, had happened, at least according to the newspaper.

! ÜBUNG 11

Übung 11: Lesen Sie weiter und unterstreichen Sie die Synonyme der Wörter in Klammern!

(1. talk, 2. preceding, 3. walk, 4. normal, 5. sure, 6. numerous, 7. feel, 8. appeared)

Before going to speak to the taxi driver, Dr Black decided to go through the area she'd seen covered with the red fog the previous night. She thought she would just stroll up and down the street, and hoped that there might be someone sitting or working outside, so that she could find out if anything out of the ordinary had been observed the previous night. Someone, she felt certain, would have seen something. But the fog covered too large an area for her to knock at every door.

Everything seemed normal and quiet as she approached the area. She walked up and down the street several times. "Something happened here last night," she said to herself. "I can sense it, but I can't tell what it was." Since no one was in the street or at the doors, Dr Black rang at a few houses. The first few seemed to be empty, as no one answered. Finally, she rang and a woman in her early thirties, around Dr Black's age, answered the door.

Though they were about the same height, the woman was almost a photographic negative of Dr Black: fair-skinned to Dr Black's dark complexion, and with light-brown hair to Dr Black's dark-brown hair.

"My name's Solina Black, I'm a doctor. I was just wondering if you noticed anything strange last night."

"No, I can't say I noticed anything strange last night. Why, did something strange happen last night?"

"There was a report of a red fog."

"A red fog?"

"And streetlamps not working."

"The city sent some men down this morning, and they repaired all of them. I wondered about that. It's the first time I remember the city fixing anything here so quickly. The lamps not working, that I heard about, but I don't know anything about a red fog."

"Well, the lamps should be working tonight. Did you happen to speak to any of your neighbours today? Did any of your neigh-

bours notice anything last night around 10 pm or so?"
"Nobody mentioned anything. Around ten you say? I probably closed the curtains around then, because I fell asleep early. I slept quite well, I did. My little girl slept until six o'clock this morning which was nice, but I didn't notice anything out of the ordinary. Is this red fog dangerous then?"

Übung 12: Welche Übersetzung stimmt? Kreuzen Sie an!

1. Die Frau wusste nichts.
   a) ☐ The woman didn't know something.
   b) ☐ The woman didn't know anything.

2. Sie stand nie vor acht Uhr auf.
   a) ☐ She never got up before eight o'clock.
   b) ☐ She didn't get up before eight o'clock.

3. Sie kannte das Mädchen, das sie fragte.
   a) ☐ She knew the girl which asked her.
   b) ☐ She knew the girl who asked her.

"I've no idea, but it is strange – and I'd like to learn more about it." Dr Black pulled out a business card and handed it to the woman. "If you or your neighbours notice anything strange or hear about anything out of the ordinary, please give me a ring. This sort of thing is of great interest to me."
"Para-, para-," the woman said, trying to read the business card.
"Parapsychologist," Dr Black said helpfully.
"And what's that, do you – "
"Wait," Dr Black interrupted. "We study things that are difficult or

impossible to explain using normal methods. A red fog is of no interest to the police, but it is of interest to me."

"Are you part of some cult?"

"No, it's not a cult. We just try to explain otherwise unexplainable phenomena, such as the red fog that was seen over this area last night."

The woman promised to call if she heard of anything, but Dr Black was fairly certain she would never hear back from her. "She thinks I'm in a cult," Dr Black said to herself. "People don't understand that this world is much more complex than they think it is. There are more forces at work here than they know about. It's not always about chasing ghosts and demons, though we do that too if necessary."

Übung 13: Welches Wort ist das „schwarze Schaf"? Unterstreichen Sie das nicht in die Reihe passende Wort!

ÜBUNG 13 !

1. strange, odd, awkward, ordinary
2. reach, leave, depart, quit
3. sort, type, manner, school
4. interrupt, interest, disturb, agitate
5. difficult, handsome, troublesome, problematic
6. faith, belief, religion, right

At 3.45 pm, Dr Black was at the *Your Car* garage.

"That's him over there," the manager said, pointing to a small Indian man sitting at a table with a cup of coffee and *The Sun* opened in front of him.

Dr Black walked over to the man and introduced herself. Though she was certainly not tall, she was a little taller than the man who stood up to speak to her. He didn't stare at her the way some men did. She was not pretty in an obvious way, but some men found her thick hair and small pointed nose attractive. For the taxi driver, her features were a bit compressed and her hair lacked the shine one sees in the hair of men and women from Asia.

"I'm looking for some information about two passengers you picked up last night. Sometime after 10 pm, I believe, you picked up a man and a woman. The man was carrying a small briefcase. They came out of a red fog that was hanging over a row of houses." Dr Black gave the address.

Übung 14: Wie spät ist es?

1. 1 am	*1 Uhr*
2. 12 pm	______
3. 12 am	______
4. 6.30 am	______
5. 10.30 pm	______
6. 2.45 am	______

The man stood silently for a moment, looking somewhere to the left of her. "Taxi drivers have many customers each night," Dr Black thought, "but he must have noticed the red fog and that should help him remember the people."

"I do remember the street with terraced houses, and I do remember the people, but I don't remember a red fog. I was a little surprised at how dark the streets were, though. I don't like dark streets, and in that area the streets are usually well-lit."

"You didn't notice a red fog? It was bright enough that you should have been able to see it clearly," she said. "The headlights on your taxi should have lit it up."

Übung 15: Übersetzen Sie die Wörter in Klammern!

"I didn't see any red fog," he (1. wiederholte) __________.

"I didn't see any fog at all."

"Can you tell me anything about the people? Do you remember where you took them?"

"Well, that's easy. I took them to Piccadilly Station. They were (2. tragen) __________ sunglasses, but in the (3. Dunkelheit) __________ I couldn't really see much else. I did think it (4. merkwürdig) __________ about the sunglasses, wearing them on such a dark night, but you get used to seeing strange things like that if you drive a taxi for long. People are strange."

"You took them to Piccadilly Station?"

"Yes. They didn't say anything on the way, so I don't know where they were going. I expect there aren't many trains coming through at that time of night though."

"If they're gone, then they're gone," Dr Black (5. dachte) __________. "I don't know if my interest in them ends right there or not. Was it a (6. Zufall) __________ that they left when they did? And why were they wearing sunglasses at night? Maybe they were trying to (7. verstecken) ______________ their faces; maybe they were on something. Many (8. Drogen) ______________ make people sensitive to light."

"And you saw nothing (9. Ungewöhnliches) ______________ in the sky last night?" she asked him once again.

"No, I didn't see anything unusual last night."

"Nothing red or orange in the sky?"

"I didn't see anything, madam."

Dr Black thanked the man and left the garage. She crossed the street to her scooter and looked back at the building. There was nothing special about it. Over it, there was only blue sky. No red fog anywhere.

"So, he didn't see the red fog last night. Maybe he's lying and trying to help cover up whatever it was that happened. Either he's part of something, or I'm the only one so far who saw the red fog last night. But he's the second person who didn't see it. Of course, the woman I spoke with earlier wasn't outside. She would have had to look out the window, and if she only closed the curtains then she probably didn't even really look outside. Clearly she would never have seen it.

And these two people who ran through the red fog. They must have seen it, but I'll never find out who they were or where they went – or if they have any connection to the phenomenon. So it's only me, at the moment. I'll have to be on the alert again tonight for the fog."

Übung 16: Beantworten Sie die Fragen zum Text!

1. What newspaper was the taxi driver reading?

___

2. Did he see the red fog?

___

3. Where did he take his strange passengers?

___

4. What was so strange about the passengers?

___

5. Did anybody else see the red fog?

___

Dr Black decided to drive over to the train station to see if any trains stopped in Manchester after 10 or 11 pm. She wandered around the old, red brick station but could not find any timetables. “There must be someone who can tell me something,” she thought. “Where are the ticket counters?” She wandered around the station, which was poorly marked, but when she saw a long queue, she knew it was people waiting to buy tickets. “This is one queue that I won’t be standing in,” she said. “I’m going home.”

Übung 17: Wie heißen die zusammengesetzten Substantive? Setzen Sie die richtige Ziffer ein!

1. ticket	☐ class
2. railway	☐ officer

3. street | counter
4. taxi | station
5. first | lights
6. police | driver

3. street	☐ counter
4. taxi	☐ station
5. first	☐ lights
6. police	☐ driver

Though the night was cold, Dr Black spent several hours outside riding her scooter in both directions along Oxford Street and Deansgate Road. She kept one eye on the road and one eye on the horizon. Something inside her told her that the fog would not reappear, but she felt it her duty to remain watchful. After several hours, however, she had seen nothing, so she decided to just go home and go to bed. "What a frustrating day," she thought, before falling asleep.

! ÜBUNG 18

Übung 18: Unterstreichen Sie die fünf inhaltlich nicht dazugehörigen Sätze!

An impatient knock at the door distracted Dr Black from a book she was reading relating practices of the ancient Celts to those of several Native American tribes in New Mexico. Instead of searching for more information on the red fog, she had decided to read about something completely different. She was a wild and crazy woman.
"What can I do for you?" Dr Black asked at the door.
"Actually, Dr Black, it's what I can do for you."
She reached for her sunglasses and put them on. A tall thin man, with thinning grey-brown hair receding from his forehead and a black hat in his hand, stood looking down towards Dr Black. She stood there in her bathing suit. If there was one thing Dr Black had learned in the last eight years of her studies and then later in her practice with Dr Grimes, it was that you cannot trust too much in

appearances. So she poured a glass of water over her head to calm herself down. Even so, she didn't like to be too trusting. The man pulled a letter from his jacket and handed it to Dr Black. "What pretty paper!" she thought.

"Let's come straight to the point, shall we? What are you trying to sell?" She stared at the letter a moment. "What?" she asked, taking the letter he was still pushing in her direction. "I'm supposed to read the letter, I suppose?"
"The letter should explain everything."
"I don't have any money to be giving away," she said.
"That isn't the nature of this call. I think you'll be pleasantly surprised."
"I do love surprises," she said, a little playfully, showing at the same time that she didn't really believe him.

Übung 19: Übersetzen Sie!

1. Sie bat den Fremden, gleich zur Sache zu kommen.

2. Sie traute dem äußeren Erscheinungsbild nicht.

3. Sein Haar wurde langsam dünner.

4. Dr. Black hasste es, abgelenkt zu werden.

5. Er zog eine Zeitung aus seiner Aktentasche.

Dr Black slowly opened the envelope and removed the letter, folding it open rather dubiously, while at the same time keeping an eye on the man in front of her. Her interest was immediately awakened by the letterhead, for it was from the University of London, which she had attended. The name in the right hand column was none other than Dr Eileen Grimes, the professor and mentor with whom she had worked quite closely during most of her stay in London. She read through the short letter twice. Though the two women had worked together for years, Dr Black had never read such a letter from her mentor. The letter in her hand was so formal that it didn't seem like the kind of letter Dr Grimes would have written to her. And yet there was something about it that reminded her of her one-time professor and associate.

Übung 20: Wie heißt die richtige Übersetzung? Ordnen Sie zu!

1. keep going	☐ sich trennen von
2. come up with something	☐ sich kümmern um
3. hold on to	☐ sich etwas ausdenken
4. show around	☐ weitermachen
5. break up with	☐ festhalten an
6. look after	☐ herumführen

"So, you are Henry Weatherly?"
"At your service," he said with a nod.
"How did Dr Grimes know that I had a servant's quarters behind my house?"

"She reckons you may need my help."
"She does, does she? I wonder what happened to birds leaving the nest and all that."
"The paranormal, as you well know, Dr Black, requires more than a keen intellect and intuition and talent, it sometimes requires muscle as well, a little force."
"And you are here to provide the muscle?"
"Do not be deceived, Dr Black. Like you, I am more than I appear to be."
"And what do you know about me?"
"That I would prefer to discuss inside."
Dr Black looked at the man for a moment, sizing him up, and then opened the door to allow him in. Eugene, waiting inside, walked to the other end of the large living room, just inside the hallway. As soon as Dr Black walked close to him, he began walking behind her, keeping a short distance from the newcomer.
Dr Black made tea and she, Henry Weatherly and Eugene sat together in the living room.

Übung 21: Was gehört zusammen? Setzen Sie die richtige Ziffer ein!

! ÜBUNG 21

1. remove	a) ☐	become active, cease to sleep, wake up
2. awake	b) ☐	be present at, go regularly to, accompany
3. provide	c) ☐	like better, favour, desire
4. attend	d) ☐	take away, get rid of, eliminate
5. require	e) ☐	need, wish to have, demand
6. prefer	f) ☐	supply, furnish, prepare

"Let's just say in conclusion, then," said Henry Weatherly, "Dr Grimes has great faith in your abilities, but she also sees you as a magnet for forces that could prove quite challenging. Mental challenges she believes you can handle, but the physical challenges are where I come in."

"And she believes I will need your help."

"Let's just say that I have been of service to Dr Grimes in the past, and when I came to her seeking some sort of employment recently she suggested you."

"I have no money to employ you and at the moment little prospect of having anything to pay you. My practice, as you may know, is just beginning here in Manchester."

"There are forces at work already, Dr Black, as Dr Grimes herself said in her letter."

"Are there indeed?" she asked.

"I've already begun to sense that myself," she said to herself, "but at the moment it's far too uncertain just what is happening."

Dr Black stood. "Would you like to see the so-called servant's quarters?"

ÜBUNG 22 !

Übung 22: Fügen Sie die Übersetzung der in Klammern stehenden Wörter ein!

They walked out to the small (1. Gebäude) ________________ that stood a short (2. Entfernung) ________________ behind Dr Black's house. From the outside, it looked a little old but in a way that only added character. She opened the door, and led Weatherly into a house with a tiny kitchen, a not much larger (3. Wohnzimmer) ________________, a bedroom and a WC. It was not in bad shape. Students had lived in it (4. gelegentlich) ________________ over the years, so it had been maintained, although not to any high standard.

"It'll do. I (5. erwartete) ____________ worse," said Weatherly. "Absentee landlords and students (6. üblicherweise) ____________ leave behind (7. Ruinen) ____________. It'll do," he said a second time, seeming to relish the moment, "though it will be plenty of work getting it into proper shape."

"Do you have anything to (8. möblieren) ____________ it? Do you even have any clothes with you?"

"The few (9. Möbelstücke) ____________ here will do until I am able to acquire what I will need. As for clothes, I took the precaution of leaving my (10. Koffer) ____________ at the train station. I didn't want to appear too presumptuous."

"I appreciate your consideration, Mr Weatherly."

"Good. Now, could I have a few pounds for a taxi, so I can pick up my suitcases?"

"Suitcases?"

"Exactly that."

While Weatherly went to the train station, Dr Black attempted to call Dr Grimes but was only able to reach her secretary, who said she was away at a conference. Dr Black and the secretary knew each other and spoke pleasantly for a few minutes.

"Do you know anything about a Henry Weatherly? Did she really send him to me without any warning whatsoever?"
"The name is familiar, but it must be from before my time with her."
"You didn't type the letter then?"
"No indeed not."
Dr Black rang off and decided to proceed with caution. The letter was in all likelihood real, and no doubt this Weatherly would turn out to be who he said he was. Still, she knew she wouldn't open up to him immediately. She would not tell him about the red fog straightaway. The appearance of the red fog and of Henry Weatherly might just be a coincidence or it might not. From long experience, Dr Black had learned that assessing coincidences required a bit of distance.

! ÜBUNG 23

Übung 23: Vervollständigen Sie die Sätze mit den angegebenen Wörtern!
(familiar, away, type, caught, likelihood, experience)

1. A secretary has to be able to ______________ quickly.
2. Eugene's behaviour is very ______________ to Dr Black.
3. Is there any ______________ of you coming to my party?
4. While Weatherly was ______________, Dr Black rang up Dr Grimes' office.
5. She had a great deal of ______________ with the paranormal.
6. The police ______________ the thief.

"There it is again, Eugene," Dr Black said, four nights after Henry Weatherly's arrival. "There's the red fog. Unfortunately, that means we have to cut our walk short." She immediately took Eugene home, grabbed her helmet and got on her scooter. The noise of the scooter starting caught Henry Weatherly's attention.
"Where are you going, Dr Black?"
"I'm going out for a ride, Weatherly."
"Isn't it a little cold and a little late for a ride? Wouldn't it be nicer during the day?"
"It is and I'm sure it would be, but I'm going now. Good evening," she said as she pulled away.
Her scooter wouldn't get her to the area over which the red fog was hanging as quickly as a taxi could, but it gave her independence: she didn't have to wait for a taxi or keep a taxi waiting for her. Dr Black was impatient at moments such as this one. A scooter isn't exactly proper, but there were times when what was "proper" simply didn't interest Dr Black.

Übung 24: Ordnen Sie die Buchstaben zu sinnvollen Wörtern!

She rode directly up Oxford Street. This night the red fog wasn't so far north in the city as it had been the last time she had seen it. In fact, she could see almost (1. timmyleedia) ____________________ that it was probably somewhere around the university, perhaps a bit north. She came to Moberly Tower and saw that the red fog was somewhere behind the University Library. Dr Black rode her scooter down a street which led onto the university campus, onto a

(2. pmtevaen) ____________ that took her around the (3. braylir) ____________ and then turned to the right. There it was, the red fog, (4. wergilon) ____________ down onto another street of houses, (5. cherstnigt) ____________ its fingers out into another area of streets. She watched again as each of the (6. retestpalms) ____________ suddenly went out with the same electric crackle she had heard once before. Sound and light seemed to suddenly (7. rappsidea) ____________ at the same time.

"If there had been any birds singing," Dr Black thought, "they would have been silenced." The fog had settled down, filling the streets. Lights in houses stayed on, but curtains were drawn. If any-one was looking out, Dr Black couldn't see a soul.

She walked to the fog and looked up. It was quite easy to see where the fog began, although not so easy to see where it ended. Plunging in, Dr Black took several steps into the fog and then stopped and looked around. The red was gone, but the night stayed just as it was and the streetlamps remained dark. Suddenly the air filled with screams. She heard men's voices, women's voices and children's voices. There was a newspaper, with a headline that would clarify everything: she could almost see it, but the screaming disturbed her too much. She couldn't concentrate. The screams grew louder and longer and became ever more pain-filled; they made the hair on the back of her neck stand up and her arms and legs trembled. When she felt the pain of the screaming people she could stand it no longer. She ran back in the direction of her scooter. Once outside the fog, the silence took over again. She turned to look at the red fog to see that it was still there. An old man turned a corner and walked into view. He was carrying an unopened can of beer.

Übung 25: Unterstreichen Sie die richtige Alternative!

1. The fog began/begun to lower slowly.
2. She saw/has seen Weatherly yesterday.
3. He came/come up to her house.
4. Dr Black got/gets scared when she heard the screams
5. She felt/feeled the pain of the screaming people.
6. An old men gone/went by.

"Excuse me, sir, do you see that?" Dr Black pointed towards the fog.

He looked in the direction in which Dr Black was pointing. "See what, miss?"

"What? That."

"The streetlamps aren't on."

"You don't see a red fog?"

"What do you mean 'a fog'? I don't see anything." The man continued on his way, but his way didn't take him into the fog and soon he passed out of sight. "People ought to have better things to do this time of night than..." she heard him mumbling as he went on his way. Dr Black was looking around, waiting for a taxi to appear, waiting for something to happen. If anything happened, though, she didn't see it. If anything happened, it was somewhere else, in some other area covered by the red fog. Suddenly the fog began to rise, to move off and away, to disappear from view. When it was completely gone, Dr Black got on her scooter and drove home.

Close to her house, she stopped, turned off her scooter and walked it up to where she parked it. A light was on in the building now occupied by Henry Weatherly, but she didn't look inside and she didn't knock on his door. She went up to her back door, stepped inside and woke up Eugene, who had been asleep in the kitchen on a large cushion that Dr Black had set up for him. There were dirty dishes in the sink, but she didn't feel like doing the washing-up. She took Eugene outside for a couple of minutes and while he sniffed around the yard, she looked up at the sky. Clouds were gathering.

! ÜBUNG 26

Übung 26: Übersetzen Sie und enträtseln Sie das Lösungswort!

1. senken _ _ □ _ _
2. schreien _ _ _ □ _ _
3. Vorsicht _ □ _ _ _ _ _
4. Versuch _ _ □ _ _ _ _
5. Geschirr _ _ _ □ _ _
6. Bürgersteig _ _ _ □ _ _ _ _
7. zittern _ □ _ _ _ _ _
8. Bibliothek □ _ _ _ _ _ _
9. Hof □ _ _ _

Lösung: _ _ _ _ _ _ _ _ _

Back inside, she thought, "I really should do those dishes."
Instead, she walked up the stairs to her bedroom. She glanced at her face quickly in the mirror, then leaned over the sink, washed her face and blindly reached for a towel to dry it. Hanging the towel up,

she noticed a faint burning on her face. Turning to leave the bathroom, out of the corner of her eye, something else caught her attention. The mirror. Leaning forward, Dr Black touched her face. It was now red, red as if sunburnt. In fact, now she noticed that her skin burned as if she had been at Brighton on the beach without wearing any sun cream. Her neck was also a bright red. Opening the top button of her shirt, she saw the burn stopped just where her clothes began. Her hands were red as well.

Übung 27: Fügen Sie die passenden Wörter ein!
(sunburn, sheets, jumped, realised, slipped, undressed, bedroom, explain)

Nothing else had been exposed, however. She walked into her 1. ______________, followed by Eugene, and 2. ______________ for bed. Eugene 3. ______________ onto her bed and lay in his usual place. As she 4. ______________ between the 5. ______________, Dr Black 6. ______________ that in the morning she would have to 7. ______________ the sunburn, if it were indeed 8. ______________, to Weatherly. "What am I going to say? It must have been that fog, but I've never heard of anyone getting sunburn from fog."

"Is that your dad living behind you?"
One of the neighbours stood in front of her house. This one had a red face, but her face was red all year round. The neighbours had

begun to ask Dr Black questions, and each question seemed to get a little more personal until now one finally had the nerve to ask just who was living in the house she had bought.

"No," she answered after a pause, "it isn't my dad. It's a friend of a friend of mine."

"Is he moving in or just staying for a while?"

"Only time will tell." She had purposely given the answer likely to provoke the least approval.

"She'll also be wanting to know about my sunburn, wondering where it came from. Same place as yours, I could say, or I could tell her I've just returned from Ibiza." The neighbour continued on her stroll, and Dr Black walked back inside her house.

ÜBUNG 28 !

Übung 28: Welche Übersetzung stimmt? Kreuzen Sie an!

1. Dr. Black sprach gestern mit Weatherly.
   a) ☐ Dr Black spoke to Weatherly yesterday.
   b) ☐ Dr Black has spoken to Weatherly yesterday.

2. Der Sonnenbrand schmerzte nicht mehr.
   a) ☐ The sunburn doesn't hurt anymore.
   b) ☐ The sunburn didn't hurt anymore.

3. Dr. Black wollte nicht mit der Nachbarin reden.
   a) ☐ Dr Black didn't want to talk to her neighbour.
   b) ☐ Dr Black wouldn't talk to her neighbour.

The sunburn – or, better still, the burn – no longer hurt, but she wasn't looking forward to her first encounter of the morning with Weatherly. She had not slept well because of the burn, and so she was not in the best of moods. Naturally, she tried to hide it, but her fatigue made that difficult. And she was also puzzled about the red fog. Two people now should have seen the fog but had not. She herself had walked inside it, and it had suddenly vanished until she again stood outside it. Was she the only person who could see the red fog? If so, why? Why should she be able to see the fog and nobody else?

Übung 29: Setzen Sie die richtige Präposition ein!
(into, up, in, on, for, inside)

1. Dr Black walked ____________ the stairs.
2. She went ____________ her living room.
3. He reached ____________ a cup of tea.
4. There was a mole ____________ her face.
5. Weatherly wanted to move ____________ with Dr Black.
6. Dr Black walked about ____________ the fog.

The phone rang and she went to answer it.
"Dr Solina Black?"
"Yes."
"This is Clare Barons."
"Yes, Ms Barons, what can I do for you?"
"Do you know who I am?"
"As my advertisement says, I'm not a mind-reader, Ms Barons, so I don't know who you are, not yet."
"I haven't seen your advertisement."
"How did you get my name then?"

"You gave me your card."
"I gave you my card?"
"Yes, a few days ago, when you dropped by my house and asked me questions about a red fog, you gave me your card. You told me if I discovered anything that I should call you, so here I am calling you."
Dr Black was suddenly completely focused. "I'm truly sorry, Ms Barons," she said. She hadn't asked the woman's name on the day she questioned her, so it was no wonder she had not recognised it.

Übung 30: Finden Sie die Synonyme und setzen Sie die richtige Ziffer ein!

1. explain	☐ appear
2. remember	☐ find out
3. hurt	☐ visit
4. seem	☐ recall
5. drop by	☐ harm
7. discover	☐ make clear

"Has something happened?"
"It turns out that the night that you saw the fog something did happen. A neighbour four houses down, Charles Gibson, has just been found half-starved. It seems his wife and her lover tied him up, robbed him and fled the city."
"Who discovered him?"
"The landlord went in to work on the stove and heard him banging around upstairs and thought maybe some animal had got into the house, a bird or something. They'd bound his mouth, tied his arms behind his back and tied his legs together, so all he could do was

bang his head against the wall. The police just left, and he's in hospital now, lucky man."

"That is news," said Dr Black. "Do you know anything about his wife? Was she a normal person?"

"She didn't seem any different from anyone else," answered Ms Barons. "But if you ask me, normal people don't go around doing what she did, do they?"

"If you find out anything of interest about her, please give me a call, Ms Barons. I'm not really interested in her affairs. I don't care that she had a lover or that she ran off with him, but if you find out more about her background that would be of interest."

"Okay." There was a pause. "I'm sorry I didn't see the fog the other night."

"You needn't apologise. If you didn't see it, then you didn't see it. You must always be honest, even if it means you have to say something you'd rather not say. Thank you for calling, Ms Barons."

"Goodbye."

Übung 31: Beantworten Sie die Fragen zum Text!

1. What did Henry Weatherly want from Dr Black?

____

2. Who gave him her address?

____

3. Why did Dr Black decide not to tell Weatherly about the fog?

____

____

4. What happened when Dr Black stepped into the fog?

5. Was Dr Black hurt by the fog?

6. How many people saw the fog?

7. What did Ms Barons tell Dr Black?

Dr Black put the phone down. “I wonder if something happened last night. Perhaps a taxi was waiting at another street, just outside the red fog again. Of course it can’t be that every place the red fog goes a woman ties up her husband, robs him and leaves him. There’s nothing to do but go back there today and go from door to door again and ask if anyone noticed anything last night.”

She went outside to get her scooter. Eugene was sitting in the back-yard observing Weatherly, who held in his hand an s-shaped metal pipe, which he was trying to clean.

“The sink is blocked-up?” Dr Black asked.

“Not too bad yet. But it was just a matter of time, so I decided to do it now before we get busy. And I expect that to happen at any time.”

Dr Black got on her scooter and was about to start it when Henry Weatherly asked, “Did you see anything interesting last night?”

“Quite possibly,” she answered.

“Remember, Dr Black. We’re a team now. I don’t intend to stay here for free. You should allow me to help you on projects where I

can be of use. Where did you get that sunburn?"
"It isn't really sunburn, Weatherly. I got it last night." She got back off the scooter and removed the helmet.

Übung 32: Was wird hier beschrieben? Ordnen Sie zu!

1. watch closely	☐	allow
2. plan to do something	☐	rob
3. take something away	☐	observe
4. have much to do	☐	intend
5. steal something	☐	remove
6. permit	☐	be busy

"Last night?" When no further explanation came, he said, "You don't trust me, do you?"
"What happened between you and your last employer?"
"We agreed," he said after a moment, "to go our separate ways."
"You came to Manchester."
"By way of London."
"And your last employer?"
"He met his final reward. He jumped through a window, after being chased by something he couldn't identify. I thought it was a simple demon, but he felt sure it was a childish prank and that there was no demon responsible. Just before he jumped, I think he knew I was right. There are many different types of demons, and I've seen what demons can do. They warm your bed up or do all sorts of things to surprise and frighten you, and then they turn your life into a nightmare. They're really most dangerous when you underestimate them. Then they can be very mean and even lethal."
"The first rule is always to learn what you're dealing with."

Übung 33: Unterstreichen Sie das „schwarze Schaf“!

1. demon, ghost, devil, demand
2. nightclub, nightmare, horror, shock
3. mean, caring, evil, bad
4. surprise, astonish, catch, amaze
5. turn, trust, belief, confidence
6. warm, cold, friendly, loving

“And that,” thought Dr Black, “is what I’m trying to decide about you. What or who are you? And are you trying to tell me something?” Dr Black got back on her scooter and started it. She was about to pull away when she said, “You should know that the neighbours have begun asking about you.”

“That’s the type of place we have here, is it? I can see we shall make our presence known. They’ll learn not to ask any questions. Or they’ll come to regret asking them. You see, I’ll give them real answers to their questions.”

“Is that a threat, Weatherly? I should like,” she said, looking at the alleyway that ran behind her house, “to have peaceful relations with my neighbours if at all possible.”

“It’s not a threat at all, Dr Black; it’s a fact, learned from long experience. As you may or may not know, I worked with Dr Grimes years ago. In her younger days, she enjoyed describing to people, who had no business knowing it at all, just what she did. Some called her mad, and others threatened to call the police. Most never really completely recovered, never saw her again as just a neighbour, just someone with an interesting profession. They looked at her as if she were the devil come back to take its own. As far as they knew, she was no longer a member of the human race.”

Übung 34: Bilden Sie aus dem Substantiv ein Verb!

1. employer ____________________
2. separation ____________________
3. explanation ____________________
4. estimation ____________________
5. surprise ____________________
6. agreement ____________________

Dr Black drove away. In a short time she was back at the street where she had seen the red fog the previous night. A Manchester City lorry was parked on the street, and two workers were replacing light bulbs.

"What happened?" asked Dr Black.

"Blowed if I know," answered the elder of the two workers. "The last few years we've had to replace light bulbs on an entire block or in an entire neighbourhood just about once a month or so. I don't know if we have a problem with the electric wiring. Can't figure it out. Nothing is broken, so it's not the young people knocking the lights out. Just every now and again, a block or two light bulbs have to be replaced."

"You replace them, and they work fine?"

"Yes, madam."

Übung 35: Bilden Sie den Satz jeweils im Simple Past!

1. They have driven away together.

____

2. She has been back from her holiday.

____

3. Only Dr Black has seen the red fog.

____

4. She has gone to bed early.

____

5. Weatherly has been very tired.

____

"This has been going on for a longer period of time then," she thought.
Dr Black walked away from the two men and started ringing doorbells at the houses. Several women answered and reported nothing strange, nothing out of the ordinary.
"I went to bed early," said one.
"I was tired and fell asleep watching BBC1," said another. "It was a fascinating documentary about the rainforest, but I just couldn't keep my eyes open."
Dr Black gave each woman her business card and then went on to the next house.

Übung 36: Verbessern Sie die falsch geschriebenen Wörter!

Two days later one of the many woman 1. ______________ she had spoken to, a Ms Helen Carter, called her.
"Mrs Nelson losed 2. ______________ her tea service. It was stolen."

"A tea service, Ms Carter?"

"It wasn't just any old tea service, Dr Black. It was a tea service given to her great-grandmother by Queen Victoria. Her great-grandfather dyed 3. ________________ for Queen and country and was a war hiero 4. ________________, so the Queen had this tea service presented to her. And now it's gone. Mrs Nelson doesn't know exactly when it was taken, but she said she felt certen 5. ________________ it was the night of the fog. Though I didn't see any fog. She remembord 6. ________________ polishing it that afternoon and putting it away in her china cabinet. This morning, she noticed it was gone."

"Are there any sospects 7. ________________? Not just anyone can get into her house, I should think, and not just anyone would know about the tea service."

"Her son's a wild young man, running with a bad croud 8. ________________. She thinks he might have taken it. Either he took it, or maybe one of his friends did."

"Thank you for calling, Ms Carter," Dr Black said. "If you learn anything more, please give me a wring 9. ________________."

"Will do, Dr Black."

"So," thought Dr Black, "this fog seems to appear wherever a crime is being committed or is about to be committed. Now, the question is, "Does it come while the crime is being committed or only afterwards? The first night, I saw the man and woman come out of the fog. They had just robbed and tied up the woman's husband, so the fog came as they were about to act – or possibly just before. The other night: it isn't clear what, if anything, happened. The tea service was probably stolen that same night. But then where does the fog come from? Is someone controlling it? And the fog isn't without side effects. The woman and her lover, did they get sunburnt? Did the son or one of his friends get sunburnt?" Dr Black decided to ring Ms Carter back.

! ÜBUNG 37

Übung 37: Bringen Sie die Wörter in die richtige Reihenfolge!

1. stolen service Mrs was Nelson's tea

....

2. from service was Victoria tea Queen the

....

3. Nelson's is young wild son man a Mrs

....

4. tea wondered she the had service son if stolen the

....

....

5. while fog committed always being a the was crime came

....

....

"Ms Carter, this is Solina Black calling back. You should ask your friend Mrs Nelson if her son or one of his friends has sunburn."
"Sunburn?"
"Yes. I was out the other night, and I saw the red fog. I decided to walk into it, and I got pretty bad sunburn, as if I'd spent a whole day at Brighton on the beach without any sun protection whatsoever."
"Red as a lobster?"
"Just so. And I'm still sunburnt. It hasn't gone away as quickly as normal sunburn."
"And you think he might be sunburnt as well?"
"I expect he is, if he went out in the fog. Tell your friend that if her son is sunburnt then he is the one who stole her tea service. If he isn't, she should tell her son that if any of his friends are sunburnt then that friend stole something of great value to their family. Maybe that would encourage him to try and get it back."
Ms Carter said she would pass on the message to her friend and would call Dr Black when she found out anything new.
"What am I doing?" Dr Black asked herself. "I have to take a more active approach. Why am I waiting for Helen Carter to do my work for me? I suppose Dr Grimes always played the active role in the past, but now it's time for me to take it over. I'll go visit this Mrs Nelson myself."

ÜBUNG 38 !

*Übung 38: Vervollständigen Sie mit **as** oder **like**!*

1. Do __________ you like.

2. She looked __________ her brother.

3. Dr Black wasn't __________ quick __________ usual.

4. It looks __________ rain.

5. Weatherly was __________ clever __________ Dr Black.

6. Dr Black felt __________ a red lobster.

7. Henry Weatherly deals with the paranormal, __________ does Dr Black.

8. The tea smells __________ strawberry.

Dr Black jumped on her scooter and went back to the neighbourhood behind the University Library. It was a warm day, so she enjoyed the ride up to the university area. "Spring, I tell you, spring is coming," she thought.

Reading the names on gate posts, Dr Black found Mrs Nelson's house.

"Mrs Nelson? I'm Solina Black, and I'm researching a mysterious phenomenon. I got word that the other night you had a tea service stolen. Is that true?"

"Who told you that?"

"One of your neighbours."

"Evelyn Goodall, no doubt. She's always got her nose where it doesn't belong."

"Never mind who told me," Dr Black said gently, "could you tell me if you are indeed missing a tea service? If so, I'd like to try and help you get it back."

"Do you work for the police?"

"Not exactly, Mrs Nelson. I work *with* the police. They sometimes request my help in solving cases that cannot be sorted out by normal police methods."

Mrs Nelson invited Dr Black inside, and they had tea.

Übung 39: Welche Bedeutung haben folgende Redewendungen? Kreuzen Sie an!

1. to lend someone a hand
   a) ☐ to cut off your hand for someone
   b) ☐ to lend someone money
   c) ☐ to help someone with something

2. not to lift a finger
   a) ☐ to lift something on one finger
   b) ☐ to watch while others work
   c) ☐ to point at someone

3. to be nosy
   a) ☐ to have a big nose
   b) ☐ to have a cold
   c) ☐ to involve yourself in the affairs of others

4. to lose your head
   a) ☐ to be punished
   b) ☐ to become irrational
   c) ☐ to lose a bet

"Three nights ago, you were at home?"
"Yes. I went to bed early. I was very tired, which is a bit unusual for me, as I've always been a night owl."
"Have you seen your son in the past two days?"
"I haven't seen him for a week, but that isn't unusual, Dr Black. He's a young lad and wants to do his own thing without his mother checking up on him every other day."
"The other night, the night your tea service was probably stolen, I

came to this part of the city because a red fog was in the sky directly overhead. It descended upon this block of houses, and the area around as well. When I walked into the fog and looked back out, it seemed that there was no fog at all, so you would probably have seen nothing had you looked out one of your windows. However, when I got home, I noticed that I had sunburn, sunburn I got while inside the fog, which means it isn't sunburn, but I don't know what else to call it at the moment."

"I can still see it on you. You got it in the fog?"

"That's right. In a red fog. I know it's hard to believe, I was terribly surprised myself, but that's the only explanation. I haven't been to Ibiza or anywhere else where you get sun this time of year."

"You didn't spend too long in a tanning studio?"

"No. I got it the other night after walking into a fog."

ÜBUNG 40 !

Übung 40: Welche Wörter haben eine ähnliche Bedeutung?

1. evidence	☐ explain
2. hint	☐ questionable
3. criminal	☐ observe
4. suspicious	☐ thief
5. solve	☐ clue
6. detect	☐ proof

"Now, your son," continued Dr Black, discreetly, "if he stole your tea service – ."

"Who said anything about my son? How did he get dragged into this? Same bunch of gossips blacking my son's reputation."

"Well, maybe he didn't steal it, but whoever did knew about it before coming into your house. And if your son did take the tea

service, then he had to go out into the fog, which means he should have sunburn as well. Do you know where he is at the moment?"
"I know where he's living at the moment, but I don't know if he's there just now."
"The sooner you see him, the better. If he has sunburn, there's probably no reason to get the police involved. You can just tell him you want the tea service back immediately."
"I would like to keep the police out of it, if I can, but I do want that tea service back as well. It's been in my family for over a hundred years now. He's not a bad boy, Richard, but he needs direction. I've tried to give it to him, but he won't hear anything from me anymore. And people round here only have bad things to say about him. But he isn't a bad boy. He's got spirit and intelligence."
"Would you like me to go with you?"

Übung 41: Wie lauten die Sätze in der richtigen Reihenfolge?

1. mother reputation defended Richard's his

2. about neighbours son her gossiped the

3. the would sunburn knew thief she have

4. Dr get beach Black not her at sunburn did the

5. mystery service she the of solved tea the

....

They took Mrs Nelson's car to her son's flat, which was on a dark and dirty street. The building was plain and square and grey, and the main door stood open, despite the cool temperature of the day. They knocked on the flat door several times and were about to leave when the door finally opened. It was Richard Nelson, looking as if he had just been awoken from a very necessary sleep.

"Mum?" he asked, and then looked at Dr Black and frowned. "What are you doing here, mum?"

Dr Black saw immediately that the son was not sunburnt. No amount of cream or make-up could have hidden sunburn on his face without being obvious. Mrs Nelson looked at Dr Black with relief.

"I just came by to see you."

"Who's that?"

"An acquaintance. Ms Black."

He reluctantly opened the door and let them in. The flat was in complete disorder. Clearly two or three people lived there, and there were so many beer cans around that it was clear that many people had been there the night before. Richard Nelson, who looked to be about 21 or 22, went into the kitchen, quickly boiled some water, then came back with three cups, each with a string from a teabag hanging out of it.

ÜBUNG 42!

Übung 42: Übersetzen Sie und enträtseln Sie das Lösungswort!

1. Gespenst _ _ ☐ _ _
2. Junge ☐ _ _

3. verhungern _ _ _ _ ☐ _
4. Zeit _ ☐ _ _
5. fallen lassen _ _ ☐ _
6. Tasse _ ☐ _
7. Fremder ☐ _ _ _ _ _ _ _

Lösung: _ _ _ _ _ _ _

"I told you he had manners," Mrs Nelson said. "Thanks, Richie." Another young man walked into the room. Richard's flatmate clearly showed signs of sunburn. Mrs Nelson's jaw dropped when she saw the boy enter the living room, and she gave Dr Black a look of surprise. With a quick and inconspicuous shake of her head, Dr Black signalled at her to say nothing. The flatmate went into the kitchen and a minute later came back out with a cup of tea and sat down. "This is Nigel, mum. He's been living here a few months now." Nigel and Dr Black looked at each other closely. The two of them had a very similar skin colour. Dr Black could see that he no longer wanted his seat in the living room, but he couldn't just get up and leave suddenly, without an explanation, not with a cup of tea in his hand.

Übung 43: Welche Gegenteile gehören zusammen? Ordnen Sie zu! !

1. polite	☐ front
2. understandable	☐ early
3. quick	☐ confusing
4. late	☐ rude
5. show	☐ hide
6. back	☐ slow

ÜBUNG 43

"Found any work, Richie?" Mrs Nelson asked.

"I'm still looking. The dole isn't enough to get by on, and I'm bored just sitting around. But there still isn't much out there. Most employers, when they see I have my 'A' levels and 'O' levels, don't want anything more to do with me. They think I must have done something to end up here."

"Like drink too much beer," Nigel added with a strained laugh, which suggested he might be suffering from a hangover.

"Have you been to Bermuda lately?" Dr Black asked him.

"Me to Bermuda? I haven't a pound to my name. What would I be doing in Bermuda?"

Übung 44: Setzen Sie die Verben in Klammern ins Simple Past!

"But you're sunburnt. You (1. not be) ____________ in a tanning studio."

"I don't really know, uh, how I (2. get) ________________ it," he (3. answer) ____________, and Dr Black could see he was telling the truth.

"Well, I do, Nigel. You got it three nights ago, as you were leaving Mrs Nelson's house. You were wearing gloves, which is why your hands aren't burned," she (4. say) __________, holding her own hands out, which were pink. "I (5. not be) ________________ wearing gloves, but I should have been. It would have saved me a bit of pain."

"I wasn't anywhere near your mum's house," Nigel said to Richard.

"I am sure you were there," Dr Black said, "and you (6. take) __________ a particularly valuable tea service."

"What?" Richard said.

"He took the tea service your grandmother (7. give) __________ me, Richie."

"Nigel, is that true?"

"You can stop playing innocent, Richie," Nigel said. "You were as much a part of it as I was."

"I really don't want to hear any more," Mrs Nelson (8. shout) __________ loudly. "Don't say another word. I don't want to see any more young men in jail. I just want the tea service back, and I want it now."

The two young men looked at each other. With their shabby clothes, their hair standing up and their faces grey from several days without shaving, they almost looked like brothers. "We pawned it, mum," Richard said after a moment.
"Then give me the money and the ticket, and I'll go get it back."
"It's not that simple. He'll charge you more to get it back," Richard said, "than he paid us for it. That's always how it goes."
"I don't mind. I just want it back. It's got to stay in the family. And since you're not interested in it, I'll be giving it to your sister. Now, give me the money and the ticket, and I'll be willing to forget the whole thing."

ÜBUNG 45 !

Übung 45: Wie heißen die zusammengesetzten Wörter?

1. bed	☐ song
2. flat	☐ keeping
3. pawn	☐ room
4. peace	☐ spoon
5. tea	☐ mate
6. folk	☐ shop

"We need the money," Nigel said to Richard as the latter went into the bedroom.

"It doesn't matter," Richard said, his voice admitting defeat. As he came back he handed his mother a ticket and some cash.

She counted the money and then asked, "This is all you got for a tea service given to my great-grandmother by Queen Victoria?"

"The people at the pawnshops, they don't care if it was given to us by Queen Victoria or Joe at the corner shop. They hear so many stories they don't believe anything you tell them anyway."

"They don't care if it was stolen or not, that's what you're saying, Richard."

"They care about two things, mum: making money and staying out of jail. Where do you think you're living?"

"We're going to go fetch the tea service," Mrs Nelson said and the two women rose and left.

ÜBUNG 46 !

Übung 46: Setzen Sie die richtigen Präpositionen ein!
(with, at, to, in, by)

Dr Black then accompanied Mrs Nelson 1. ______ the pawnshop where, 2. __________ a bit of haggling and threatening, the two women got the tea service back without spending too much money.

"I'm just glad to have this back," she said, holding the box containing the tea service. "It'll need to be cleaned again, look 3. _____ all the fingerprints, but I don't mind that."

"Do you mind if we drop 4. _____ your son's flat again quickly? Only this time I want you to remain outside. I need to speak to the two of them briefly. Especially Nigel."

Dr Black rang the doorbell and Richard answered the door again.

"What?" he asked, not impolitely, but instead like a little boy tired of being told he's done wrong. "He wouldn't give mum the tea service back?" he guessed, sticking his head through the crack 5. _____ the door.

"Never mind that, she has it already. I'd like to speak to you and Nigel briefly." He made no move to open the door wider. "I think you would prefer if I spoke to you inside rather than out here where the neighbours might hear."

"Our reputation isn't likely to get any worse. Nigel's out," he said, opening the door so Dr Black could walk in.

"Did you and Nigel come up with the idea to steal your mother's tea service, or are you working with someone else?"

"It was Nigel's idea. He once asked if my mum had anything worth stealing and I told him about it. I thought it was just a joke at the time. I went along with it, but I never really thought it would happen. I thought something would come up in between, maybe he and

I would find work, and we wouldn't really have to do it. But he really did it."

"So you two were working on your own, not for anyone else?"

"Who else would we work for? We just need money for rent and food and beer."

Dr Black thanked Richard and left.

"He isn't such a bad boy," Mrs Nelson said, driving back to her house.

"He isn't," Dr Black agreed. "It's just a hard time to be on the dole. One of these days, the economy will get better."

"Maybe if we had the Euro."

"Maybe."

! ÜBUNG 47

Übung 47: Vervollständigen Sie die Fragen mit einem passenden Fragewort!

1. __________ did Nigel go?
2. __________ stole the tea service?
3. __________ did he do with it?
4. __________ did Dr Black get sunburnt?
5. __________ form of transportation do you prefer?
6. __________ was Nigel nervous?

"It's just as I feared," Dr Black thought, putting her helmet on and getting onto her scooter. "There's no connection between the crimes committed when the red fog is around. There's no connection at all – at least not yet. But who or what's responsible for the fog, that's what I need to sort out first. Is this fog a warning that there's a robbery or a crime of some sort being committed or is it a way of assisting the crime? The few people I've spoken to, they all say they were asleep around the time when I observed the fog. And these crimes are always committed early in the night, not at 3 or 4 am, when people are normally fast asleep. And both nights were during the week, not at the weekend. The first night was a Wednesday and the second night a Monday."

Übung 48: Welche Wörter gehören in die Lücken?
(hit, moving, get, drove, pulled, turned, noticed)

Dr Black started her scooter and 1. ____________ out into the street. She had just got going when a lorry seemed to appear out of nowhere. She 2. ________________________ immediately that it was 3. _________________ too fast for the road and was coming straight at her. There wouldn't be enough room for the two of them. Just before the lorry would have 4. _____________ her, Dr Black quickly 5. ____________ between two parked cars and watched it go past. She had just narrowly missed being hit. She pulled onto the pavement and 6. ____________ even faster to the end of the street, then headed back towards Oxford Street. "Just a coincidence?" she wondered. She turned right and saw that the street had been closed off. "I reckon I'll 7. ____________ to Oxford Street another way," she thought, and drove in the other direction, a little faster now than she might have if she hadn't had the near run-in with the lorry.

She turned into another street and the lorry suddenly came up behind her again. It was pulling up quickly towards her. “No coincidence here,” she thought solemnly. “Can’t outrun a lorry, not on a scooter and not on a road.” Dr Black had only seconds to react. The lorry driver was without a doubt trying to hit her. She could feel the warmth of the engine on her back as the lorry drew nearer. She was about to panic, when suddenly an entrance to a car park opened like a hungry mouth, and she turned in. Just barely managing to keep her balance, she crossed the entrance and drove onto the pavement again. This time, however, she remained on the pavement, cutting between several buildings until she found herself on the campus of the University of Manchester. Speeding between offices and classroom buildings, she lost sight of the lorry. More importantly, the lorry driver lost sight of her. Rather than turning immediately towards Oxford Street again, she drove towards Whitworth Park, driving as fast as she dared on the nearly empty pavements. She stopped between two rows of flats for Manchester University students and waited for a moment. Her heart was beating furiously.

ÜBUNG 49 !

Übung 49: Übersetzen Sie die folgenden Substantive!

1. LKW ______________________
2. Büro ______________________
3. Fußgänger ______________________
4. Fahrer ______________________
5. Eingang ______________________
6. Geschwindigkeit ______________________

"So," she thought, "I seem to have made myself known to someone. Might Nigel have something to do with this? He was gone, after all, when I went back and spoke with Richard Nelson." She sat still for a moment, breathing deeply and calming herself. "Do I go home via Oxford Street or do I avoid it?" she wondered. "On Oxford Street, he could follow me and find out where I live, if I lead him to my house – but he wouldn't attack me, there would be too many witnesses. If I'm not on Oxford Street, I'm open to further attacks and I cannot outrun a lorry on this thing." She looked down at the speedometer, which only went up to 50 miles per hour. "On the other hand, he might not be able to find me, in which case I'm safer."

Übung 50: Beantworten Sie die Fragen zum Text!

1. Why was the tea service so dear to Mrs Nelson?

2. Why did Richard's friend steal the service?

3. Who does Dr Black suspect might be driving the lorry?

4. What happens each time the fog appears?

5. How did Dr Black identify the person who stole the tea service?

....

Dr Black drove up to Oxford Street and looked to the right where she expected her pursuer might be. “No lorry, at least not the one that was after me,” she thought. To the left she saw nothing either. She went south, quickly, on Oxford Street, but pulled off into Hulme and took side roads down to Didsbury. She kept her eye in the rear-view mirror and even looked over her shoulder, frequently, to make sure she was not missing anything, but no one seemed to be following her anymore. She pulled up behind the small house where Weatherly now lived and switched off the engine.

“Did you find out anything?” Weatherly asked, emerging from the house.

“No, nothing at all,” she answered, a bit angrily, as if to say, “why don’t you mind your own business?” She placed her helmet on the seat and looked at him crossly.

Weatherly stiffened a moment, frowned at her, put his hands on his hips, and then went back inside.

! ÜBUNG 51

Übung 51: Unterstreichen Sie die sieben Wörter, die falsch geschrieben sind!

Henry Weatherly walked into Dr Black’s kitchen. She was seated at her kitchen table, with a cup of tee in front of her, staring at the wall. It was a bear wall in need of colour and the one lonely picture, a cheep copy of Van Gogh’s *Starry, Starry Night,* wasn’t enough.

“Knock, please,” she said.

Weatherly knocked twice on the table in front of him. Dr Black looked up at him, angrily.

"I could smell the fear on you, Dr Black, when you got home a little while ago. What happened?"
"You can smell fear?"
"More or less: it smells like sweat to most pieple. I don't since it anymore now. You seam to have got over whatever it was that happened." Dr Black sat silently. "I can't werk with you if you won't let me. It's as simple as that. I can't assist you, if you won't let me."
"I didn't ask for your assistance."
"I know you didn't, but Dr Grimes asked me to help you."
"Well …"

"You know Dr Grimes well enough to know that she doesn't recommend people in whom she doesn't have complete faith. She told me that you were the only pupil of hers who she ever thought might be a colleague. That is why she broke off your working relationship. A mentor can inhibit growth, and she believed you had outgrown her. I'm not saying that she thinks you are better than her. She just thought that you needed other experiences. You need to learn how others work and to be free to discover how you work best. She said she had never worked with anyone as closely as she did with you, and you helped her make progress in her career. Now, in order for you to progress, you have to work on your own or with someone else. It may just be that I am that someone else."
"You're not even a parapsychologist, Weatherly. How can you even compare yourself to her?"
"I'm not foolish enough to compare myself to her. What I have that you don't have is one thing and one thing only: experience."
"What do you mean I don't have experience? I had several years of experience with Dr Grimes."
"I have more. I may not have all your gifts, but I have experience."

Übung 52: Welches Wort ist das „schwarze Schaf“? Unterstreichen Sie das nicht in die Reihe passende Wort!

1. growth, progress, regret, advancement
2. foolish, unwise, silly, clever
3. none, several, some, numerous
4. present, gift, talent, ability
5. learn, report, discover, find

There was a pause in the conversation and then Weatherly began to speak again. “So, what happened this afternoon that shook you so?”

“I wasn’t shaken.”

“You were. I know it, you know it and it isn’t a bad thing to be shaken once in awhile. It keeps you on your toes.”

“If you will know then, a lorry tried to run me over, not once but twice. I don’t know if it was a coincidence, I don’t know if it was only a warning or if the driver really did want to kill me. In any case, I’m much more mobile on my scooter than any lorry is, so I easily escaped once I got off the street. It was a narrow escape, though.”

“Can you tell me why anyone would try and kill you? And perhaps you ought to begin at the beginning.”

Übung 53: Wie lauten die Sätze? Bringen Sie die Wörter in die richtige Reihenfolge!

1. run by almost lorry the over was woman a

....

2. away new trust she people did right not

3. the instincts criminal on she her to relied find

4. hoped the to she solve mystery

5. Manchester much Weatherly not too city for care of the did

6. solving his valuable was mystery a experience in tool the

Dr Black began with the red fog of just over a week earlier and then concluded with the visit, with Mrs. Nelson, to the two young men, telling Weatherly everything she knew.

"I don't know what my next step is. Do I go out tonight and ride around the city, looking for the red fog? Do I hunt it down or do I just look up in the sky from here and if I see it, I go and follow it, and if not then I assume it isn't out?"

Eugene wandered into the room and looked up at Dr Black.

"I think," said Weatherly, "that the first step should be a walk with Eugene." Eugene whined as if he had understood and his ears went back, in proper begging style.

Übung 54: Übersetzen Sie und enträtseln Sie das Lösungswort!

1. gleich _ _ □ _
2. deins □ _ _ _ _
3. retten □ _ _ _
4. Nacht _ _ _ _ □
5. fahren _ _ _ _ □
6. Stunde _ _ _ □
7. Geschichte _ _ _ _ □

Lösung: _ _ _ _ _ _ _

"If I am to go with you, which I really believe to be a good idea," he said, walking alongside Dr Black and Eugene, "then we cannot go on your scooter. Though I would fit on the back, I would prefer not to use that form of transportation. We could, however, take a taxi for a couple of hours and drive around the city." Seeing Dr Black about to object to the cost of hiring a taxi, he added, "We could also hire a car for a couple of days. It is probably too late to hire one for tonight, however, as most of these places probably close at 6 pm and it is now nearly 7 pm."
"I can get a receipt and include it in my business expenses," Dr Black said, agreeing to the idea of a taxi.

That night they spent about two and a half hours, until 11.30 pm, driving around the city. They drove repeatedly to Piccadilly Gardens from where, Dr Black insisted, she had the clearest view of the city. Buildings were a little distant and the sky was much more open here. They saw nothing, however, and they felt inhibited by the driver: they didn't want to tell him what they were looking for.

They whispered back and forth, discussing directions to explore. In the end, they crossed the city several times, sat in Piccadilly Gardens twice and, after making one last sweep of the city, turned towards Didsbury.

Übung 55: Übersetzen Sie!

ÜBUNG 55 !

1. Zug ______________________
2. Flugzeug ______________________
3. Auto ______________________
4. Fahrzeug ______________________
5. U-Bahn ______________________
6. Fahrrad ______________________

"Well, that was less than successful," Dr Black said.

"I don't know about that," Weatherly answered. "Just because we didn't find anything doesn't mean it wasn't successful. It may also mean that there wasn't anything to be found."

"I mean," she said, opening her front door and inviting him in to pass through her house to his, "I mean that we have discovered no more about this fog, we know nothing more about it than we knew before."

"Perhaps there is nothing to discover," Weatherly said provokingly.

"I don't believe that for a second, and I don't think you do either. If we know one thing for certain, it is that this red fog is no natural phenomenon."

"Somebody controls it then."

"The thing we have to do is discover who is controlling it, how this person is controlling it and, most importantly, why."

"And how do we do that?"

"The fog simultaneously helps criminals and marks them. Which is the primary effect? In the fog, I heard screaming. I heard screams of people of all ages, horrible screams, screams of pain and misery."

"Are they possibly victims of something?"

"If they are, the fog may very well be on the side of the victims."

"Or the fog might be what made the people victims. The most important thing, at this point, is to be asking the right questions."

"Are we?"

"That's a good question."

ÜBUNG 56 !

Übung 56: Welche Gegenteile gehören zusammen?

1. success	☐ opening
2. someone	☐ something
3. natural	☐ no one
4. nothing	☐ against
5. closing	☐ failure
6. for	☐ artificial

Dr Black sat in the passenger seat while Henry Weatherly drove their hired Ford Escort towards Salford.

"I'd have chosen the Austin Martin," Weatherly was saying. "That's the preferred automobile of secret agents. What this car lacks in excitement, it makes up for in a wealth of dullness," he said, an ironic smile crossing his face.

"Let's go back to Manchester proper," Dr Black said. "I have a feeling that tonight we're going to see something."

"If we don't, I suggest you speak with that young lad, Nigel, again. I think he knows something about what's going on."

"I don't know," Dr Black answered. "I think the two crimes that I have been a witness to were unrelated."

"Or you just don't know how they are related."

"There. There it is. On the horizon. Turn left here. Don't you see it?"

"No. What?"

"Left here. Now keep straight on."

Übung 57: Formulieren Sie die Sätze im Passiv!

1. The woman and her lover tied up the man

____

____

2. Only Dr Black saw the fog.

____

3. Weatherly and Dr Black followed the fog across Manchester.

____

____

4. Dr Black made a difficult decision.

____

5. Dr Grimes sent Weatherly to Dr Black.

____

They were driving down major streets and turning down side streets in areas of Manchester neither of them had explored before.

They came to a corner, and there Dr Black watched the fog settle, lowering over a broad square of buildings and many surrounding it.
"Do you see it?"
"I see nothing, Dr Black. Do you mean that you see the red fog there?"
"I see it like I see you."
"That's some thick fog. What do we do next?"
"Get out of the car." They left the car. Following Dr Black's lead, they walked towards the red fog, which looked wet like rain and red like a brilliant sunset. "It's a shame you can't see this, Weatherly. It's really beautiful."
"You think someone might try to escape from here?"
"I'm sure someone will."
"Then we should try to find vantage points where we can see people entering or leaving the fog."
"It's too big even for two people. We need to split up."
Dr Black entered the fog. Immediately she heard the screams again. This time, she felt a burning on her skin immediately. After only a couple of minutes, she could feel bubbles forming on her hands and her cheeks. "Blisters," she thought. She ran back towards Weatherly.

ÜBUNG 58 !

Übung 58: Lesen Sie weiter und unterstreichen Sie die sechs Adverbien!

"I don't think going back into the fog again would be very wise," he said to her. "You're badly burned. I could see the fog for just a moment, however, when you entered it and when you left it. Let's split up, like you said. You call me if you need my help."
Dr Black told him where to go, and he entered the fog, walking

through it to the point where she told him to stop. Whether he was outside the fog or not, Dr Black couldn't be certain. They waited and waited, Dr Black hiding behind a tree, Weatherly crouched between two cars.

Suddenly, they saw two people emerging, two men, and they were moving towards Weatherly. Dr Black quickly started walking towards them. Weatherly waited until they were close to him, then he stood and approached them. The men charged at him immediately. If he had only had one of the men to deal with, he would have handled the fight easily. The two men, however, were a challenge. Dr Black ran towards the three men as fast as she could. Luckily, she had had thorough training in self-defence, so she and Weatherly were able to overpower the two men without great effort. Though he had been losing the fight, Weatherly had managed to keep the men from reaching for their handguns, which Dr Black then removed upon her arrival. Pointing one at the two men, she began questioning them.

"Who are you working for?" she asked

"We're not working for anyone," a tall one, with dark curly hair answered. The other one, blond, was touching his bleeding lip, where Dr Black's foot had hit him. His breathing was a little husky, and Dr Black feared she might have cracked his ribs.

"On the other hand," she realised, "the injury would keep him from moving."

"Who is helping you?" Dr Black asked. "Who did you pay to allow you to commit your robbery? I don't know how to use this, so I'm likely to shoot you by accident at any moment," she said.

"I'm not telling you anything. You're not the police or if you are, show me your ID."

"And even if you are in the police, we're not telling you anything."

ÜBUNG 59 !

Übung 59: Vervollständigen Sie die Sätze mit dem passenden Adjektiv!

(injured, brave, handsome, scary, dangerous, beautiful)

1. A film with monsters and evil people is ______________.
2. People with guns are ______________.
3. Someone with broken ribs is ______________.
4. A good-looking man is ______________.
5. A good-looking woman is ______________.
6. A person not afraid to face the unknown is ______________.

Dr Black called the police on her mobile phone. The dark-haired man stood up just as she rang off with the police, and Dr Black shot the pistol straight up in the air. The man dropped to the ground, and the two men waited peacefully until the police arrived.

Weatherly explained what had happened, leaving out the part about the red fog, and the two bobbies searched the men, finding a fistful of jewellery and a couple of small bags of white powder. Rather than thanking Dr Black and Weatherly, however, the bobbies told them they didn't require their help.

"You're a danger to yourselves, and you could become a danger for us. You'll just make our job harder. Please stay home and get your thrills watching detective shows on television. Watch *Fawlty Towers* or something to entertain you, but don't try and do our jobs. We're specially trained for this, and, believe me, the training is necessary."

"I," said Weatherly, "am Henry Weatherly. I have worked with the police in London and New York and Bangkok."

"You're in Manchester now, Mr Weatherly, and we can manage our job without your help, so please do us a favour and stay out of our way. Do please go home."
"You might as well tell us," the other bobby said, addressing the two prisoners, "which house you robbed. We'll all of us get to bed a bit sooner if you do."
Dr Black and Weatherly walked away from the scene. Weatherly was feeling particularly insulted but attempted not to show it.
"Is the fog still there?" Weatherly asked.
"No. I don't know when it rose, but it's gone now."
"We'll have to see to those burns."

Übung 60: Unterstreichen Sie die vier inhaltlich nicht passenden Sätze!

Several nights later, they saw the red fog once more. It was dancing around to loud music.
"I never thought of Manchester as a dangerous place to live," Weatherly said.
"It isn't. I think the fog is affecting people, making them commit robberies and other crimes. British people like sun. I don't know if it's bringing out the worst in them or merely providing them an opportunity to practice their undesired skills."
Despite the burns she had received the last time, Dr Black once again walked into the red fog. As with the previous times, she immediately heard screams, loud screams, furious, fear-filled screams. They wondered what on earth had happened to Winston Churchill. "Where is it happening?" she asked herself. "Is there any sign anywhere? Are the screams just a distraction, to keep me from being able to concentrate on anything else?" For a moment,

suddenly, she felt almost as if she were in water. The main meal is served around 6 pm. The fog became thicker, so that she could feel it on her skin. It was a strong burning sensation. And then she knew. An image popped into her mind, and she knew what the person looked like, the person who was responsible for the fog. She knew nothing else, but she knew what he looked like: a dark, thin moustache, dark hair with grey sprinkled throughout. She didn't know where to find the man and she didn't know why he was producing the fog, but she knew he was responsible for it.

"Should we split up and see if we can capture our lawbreaker or lawbreakers?" Weatherly asked, as she walked out of the fog up to him.

"No, the police don't want our help, and this time we're going to see if we can follow the fog."

"You don't think it will lead us back to whoever is responsible for it, do you?"

"I'm not sure what I expect. But I do expect something."

They sat in the car and waited. Another car drew up and someone ran from a house through the fog to the car. The car pulled away, disappearing quickly and very shortly afterwards the fog began to lift. Weatherly followed Dr Black's directions, and they travelled across Manchester behind the fog.

ÜBUNG 61 !

Übung 61: Bilden Sie die Kurzform!

"Do you think it's going to land somewhere else?"

"I do not (1.) ____________ know, Weatherly. But I think something is going to happen."

"Are you prepared for it?"

"That's why you are (2.) ________________ here, isn't it? Are you not (3.) ______________________ the muscles?"

"Some things even I can't defend against."

"So we are (4.) ______________ not prepared for it, but we cannot (5.) __________ prepare for something of this nature, because whatever it does will probably be a surprise. The point is to be ready for anything and to be able to think on your toes, that's what Dr. Grimes always said. Turn right here. It is (6.) ______________ stopping over this square white office building. Do you think people live there? Is it going to descend once again?"

"You have to tell me. You're the only one who can see it, remember?"

"It's settling, but it's going no lower than the top of the building," Dr Black said, ignoring Weatherly, who didn't realise she was only thinking out loud. They waited for some twenty minutes, trying to decide if they should go inside.

"Now, it seems to be rising. Why does it come here to this building only to float up and vanish? Is it just a coincidence? Is this where the person producing the fog lives or works? Is this where the fog will come tomorrow night or the next time it appears? It's gone now, the fog."

"Let's go over to the building and see what we can find out about it," Weatherly suggested.

Dr Black nodded in agreement.

Übung 62: Welche Wörter passen inhaltlich zusammen?

1. office	☐ weather
2. time	☐ building
3. fog	☐ season
4. spring	☐ clock
5. police	☐ feeling
6. fear	☐ order

They walked up to the building and looked at the brass plates next to the main doors. Several solicitors had their offices in the building and other parts of it appeared to be empty, for there were vacant spaces for nameplates.

"If a solicitor is responsible for this fog, why?"

"That doesn't explain anything to us, does it?" Weatherly asked. "Unless it's a solicitor who has become cynical about the whole system. Many people claim that solicitors just get guilty people out from behind bars and that their job is nothing more than finding some way to keep their clients out of jail. Perhaps here's a solicitor who wants to brand criminals."

"Brand them?"

"Yes. Turn them red. Mark them so that the police can find them without difficulty. Consider the two men from the other night. They weren't caught red-handed. They were caught red-faced, which is quite as bad, I should think, if you know what you're looking for."

Übung 63: Ordnen Sie die Buchstaben zu einem sinnvollen Wort!

"The (1. lpmrobe) __________ with that theory is that he isn't working with the (2. eclopi) __________," Weatherly said. "This Nigel is walking the (3. ettessr) __________. Only the two men from the other (4. thing) __________, the ones we managed to round up, they're the only ones so far who face the prospect of punishment. The rest have gone on about their (5. nubesssi) __________ with a (6. uurnnsb) __________ that will eventually go away."

"Then perhaps it's a (7. torcisoli) __________ who wants to help the (8. alscrmnii) __________, and they're paying him for his assistance. That's been one of my theories from the very beginning, that someone was helping people commit crimes."

"You're forgetting one (9. night) __________, Dr Black. You are the key here. Only you, so far, can see the fog. Why is that? Do you have some (10. laiceps) __________ talent or skill that allows you to see the fog or have you been chosen?"

"Me, chosen to see the fog? Why?"
"Well, if you were chosen, that is a mystery, isn't it? It may only be that you are the equal to whoever is responsible for the red fog and therefore you are able to see it."
"It could also be incompetence. Whoever is responsible simply doesn't think he has anyone to fear. He feels he is all-powerful and doesn't know that there's someone out there who is capable of seeing his weaknesses. That is what I really think we're facing."
"Such people are also dangerous, however. They don't know their own strengths and weaknesses, and they take on too much. They're a danger to themselves and to others."

Übung 64: Setzen Sie die Verben in Klammern ins Simple Past!

The notion of being selected (1. distress) __________ Dr Black, though she (2. be) ________ not really conscious of it. "What if it is not me who was selected," she (3. think) __________, in one of the moments when she directly thought about it, "what if it is not me who was selected but simply my abilities which selected me? It's pure chance then. I just happen to live in Manchester now. If I were in London this would be going on as usual, and nobody would be any wiser. The person replacing the lights in the streetlamps the other day (4. say) ___________ such occurrences had been happening for years. I wasn't selected by whoever is doing this. My abilities are responsible."

Rather than thinking herself to be the key figure, as Weatherly seemed to suggest, Dr Black (5. begin) ___________ to wonder if the key element were not, instead, the voices.

"Maybe," she thought, "the red fog is not something that is controlled by someone in Manchester, or in England or the UK for that matter. Maybe there's some other force at work? This is nothing like the work I had with Dr Grimes. She always seemed to know exactly what we were dealing with. Maybe it's because she was helping me too much that she wanted me to go on my own. I have to learn to detect the real issues. Weatherly and I have only come up with questions. It's been several weeks, and I have no answers at all. I had that one image of a man with a moustache, and since then I've had nothing more that has suggested any further steps."

Dr Black decided to visit the building above which the red fog had vanished. She would go from one office to another and see if any of the solicitors resembled the person she had so clearly seen. She took her scooter up to the city centre and then to the building. She drove in a circle around it, studying it from the outside. "A hungry-looking building," she thought. "It doesn't look like a place where highly successful solicitors locate their practices. They're either on their way up or on their way down when they move into these premises."

Übung 65: Wählen Sie die richtige Alternative aus!

1. Dr Black and Dr Grimes worked together
   a) ☐ as police officers.
   b) ☐ in London.
   c) ☐ for three years.

2. Weatherly cannot see the fog because
   a) ☐ he is not wearing his glasses.
   b) ☐ he is driving.
   c) ☐ he doesn't have the ability.

3. The fog travels
   a) ☐ all over England.
   b) ☐ to places where Dr Black wants it to go.
   c) ☐ to the scenes of crimes.

4. People who walk in the red fog
   a) ☐ get sunburnt.
   b) ☐ go crazy.
   c) ☐ run after taxis.

5. Dr Black and Weatherly don't
   a) ☐ even know which buttons to push.
   b) ☐ know if they're asking the right questions.
   c) ☐ know where to hire a car.

The front door opened quietly and she looked around the ground floor. None of the offices here was occupied. Though there was a lift, she went up the stairs to the first floor. Here, a solicitor's office had its door open, and Dr Black stepped up to the youngish secretary staring at a computer screen. The frequent clicking of the mouse suggested to Dr Black that the woman was playing solitaire rather than working.

With a surprised look on her face, the woman said, "How may I help you?" while at the same time clicking loudly on the mouse, no doubt to hide the game she had been playing.

"A friend of mine," Dr Black began, realising that she had not prepared an answer to this most basic of questions, "a friend of mine said she once had help on a rather strange case from a solicitor who worked in this building. Unfortunately, she couldn't remember his name. She knew only that he had a moustache and that he was no older than forty."

"Mr Flowers is a good man but he has no moustache and the cases we handle are seldom strange. We handle contracts and international business."

"Do you know of anyone who works in this building who fits this description?" Dr Black asked.

The woman thought for a moment, and then suggested that there was perhaps someone on the third – or was it the fifth? – floor who might possibly match the description. In any case, there was no point in going beyond the fifth floor, because the last three were abandoned.

Übung 66: Bilden Sie die Ordnungszahlen!

1. one ……………………
2. two ……………………
3. three ……………………
4. four ……………………
5. twenty ……………………
6. twenty-two ……………………
7. ninety-nine ……………………

"The lift stops at the fifth floor," she said, "so not to worry. You can't go up by accident."
"That's nice to know," Dr Black said. "And all the more reason to go up there," she thought, and then thanked the woman for her time.

Dr Black wandered around the first floor and then the second, looking into each office but not speaking to anyone, looking for pictures of the people who worked there, sometimes finding them, usually not. "Why so shy?" she wondered. "I have my face in the newspaper. You think they might at least have theirs in their offices." On the third floor and again on the fifth floor, Dr Black repeated her story, but when she asked for details about the solicitors' appearances, they failed to meet the description she had in mind. Four out of seven had moustaches, which was promising. Unfortunately, they were either blonde or grey but not dark-haired and pale.

! ÜBUNG 67

Übung 67: Stimmen die folgenden Aussagen? Markieren Sie mit richtig ✔ oder falsch – !

1. The building has only one storey. ☐
2. None of the solicitors has a moustache. ☐
3. The lift does not go beyond the fifth floor. ☐
4. The secretary is working hard. ☐
5. Dr Black thinks that the person whose image appeared in her head works in the building. ☐
6. Dr Black was scared to walk into the building. ☐
7. Dr Black spoke to many people. ☐

Finally Dr Black reached the three abandoned floors as described by the secretary on the first floor. She decided, naturally, that she had better explore the top three floors in order to leave no stone unturned. "This," she thought, "is probably when I should have Weatherly by my side, but if it really is abandoned then there's nothing to fear. Well, now's the time."
She climbed the stairs which, since they went along the side of the building, benefited from the outside light which was quickly fading. Up she went, to the sixth floor. She walked through the hallway, looking into each office. Some were locked, but she could

look through the glass doors into rooms containing a few pieces of furniture. These offices were clearly not inhabited. Other rooms were open and had been raided, perhaps by those in the other offices below. Desk drawers were open, papers were spread on the floor: it was chaos. In these offices, the chairs were gone, the walls were bare and the smell of failure seemed to hang in the air. On the seventh floor, she found a similar state of affairs. Most of the offices, however, had been left open. Dr Black wandered into each, explored all the rooms but again found nothing at all that helped her.

Übung 68: Übersetzen Sie!

1. Sessel ______________________
2. Schreibtisch ______________________
3. Schublade ______________________
4. Akte ______________________
5. Gardinen ______________________
6. Schrank ______________________

Though these last two floors had been empty and nothing surprising had appeared, Dr Black walked the steps up to the eighth floor with a feeling of uneasiness. As on the other floors, she looked into every office. In contrast to the others, however, the eighth floor was a little darker. The air, too, was thicker, as if this floor had even less fresh air than the two below. The curtains were drawn, though the same chaos was observable in the offices on this floor. "Perhaps here," she thought, "it is even more chaotic." She found files thrown about here and there, but did not look closely at them. "One wonders," she said to herself, "if the occupants made a hasty exit."

Übung 69: Unterstreichen Sie die richtige Alternative!

(1.) In/Into several of the offices, she pulled the curtains back to look at Manchester. "(2.)There's/Theirs the Arndale Centre," she thought, "and, well, there's nothing to be done about it now. It's here to stay, no matter how (3.) beautiful/ugly and how out of place. And there's Piccadilly Gardens. There's the train station. Over there, in the distance, is UMIST and (4.) before/beyond that Manchester University and (5.) anywhere/somewhere well beyond that, Didsbury, with Eugene and Weatherly. Those (6.) too/two," she thought, momentarily distracted (7.) for/from the task at hand, "it'll be interesting to see what develops (8.) between/among those two."

She walked the hallways once again and found another set of stairs leading upwards. "There must be a penthouse office," she thought. "I wonder if it's open. Now I wish Weatherly were here. This feels illegal as well as risky and foolish." The stairs took her to a door, which turned out to be locked. Dr Black tried it a couple of times, and then, feeling even more foolish, she knocked. Nothing happened. "What were you expecting?" she asked herself. "Did you think you would hear footsteps and then someone would open the door?"

She started to go back down the steps, when she felt a strong desire, perhaps even a need, to enter the office on the top floor. She went back up, tried the door again and found it was still locked. "No surprise," she muttered. "I'm almost on the ninth floor. Who will hear me from here?" Dr Black kicked the door several times and saw that it was weak. “I can get in there,” she thought. “I can do it.” She put her shoulder to the door and, after several attempts, suddenly found herself lying on the floor of a large office.

Übung 70: Welche Wörter haben eine ähnliche Bedeutung?

1. foolish	☐ try
2. knock	☐ stairs
3. attempt	☐ stupid
4. almost	☐ storey
5. steps	☐ tap
6. floor	☐ just about

Like the other offices on the floors directly below, this office was empty and a mess, and, like those on the eighth floor, it was also dark. It was not so dark, however, that she could not see that there were couches and chairs for clients and, in the centre, a desk – for a secretary, no doubt. This office was much larger than those below, and there were also three closed doors. She walked over to the two closed doors that were next to each other. They opened into conference rooms, each with a glass wall staring out blindly onto the city.

The third door opened into the largest room. The desk at the distant end of the room made it clear that it was the solicitor’s office. In contrast to the other offices, this one felt lived in, used, and felt as though it had recently been used. “But there’s a layer of dust covering everything,” Dr Black thought, “so it can’t have been used that recently.” There were copies of paintings on the interior walls but nothing that gave character to the offices. “A solicitor’s penthouse office. This fellow must have been living the good life. His customers knew where their money was going, at least." The furniture was from an earlier decade, but it was not that old, not so old that it was the furniture of a solicitor who had been working for decades and who had turned grey while carrying out his work.

! ÜBUNG 71

Übung 71: Ersetzen Sie die in Klammern stehenden Personen mit den richtigen Pronomen!

1. (Dr Black) __________ has a red scooter.
2. (Weatherly) __________ gave Eugene a bone.
3. Mrs Nelson loved (Richie) __________ with all her heart.
4. "(Weatherly and I) __________ have got to discover the cause of the red fog."
5. (Nigel and Richard) __________ stole the tea service.
6. The fog gave (Nigel and Dr Black) __________ sunburn.

She walked back to the secretary's desk and saw a copy of the Manchester newspaper on it. The paper was six years old. In the local headlines, which began halfway down the first page, she saw a picture of a young man she recognised. The picture in the newspaper seemed to be the exact picture that had suddenly appeared in her thoughts several nights before: a man of about forty with a pencil-thin moustache and dark, short hair parted on one side. He was a solicitor who had jumped to his death. "So, that's who he was," she said to herself. "Why, then, did I get an image of him in my head? I never saw him when he was alive, so why suddenly all these years after his death? Can he have anything to do with this fog? I think I can be excused for doubting it. But that doesn't help me to answer the question of why, six years after he fell to his death, an image of him suddenly popped into my head."

Übung 72: Fügen Sie die passenden Wörter ein!
(subjects, evening, born, article, newspaper, note, law)

She quickly read through the 1. ________, which provided just the basic facts. John William Johnson. Solicitor. 2. ________ in Stoke-on-Trent. Practising in Manchester for the last eight years. Jumped to his death Thursday afternoon. In the rain. Died immediately. "No mention of a suicide 3. ________," thought Dr Black, "so apparently he left behind nothing to explain his final act." Dr Black looked up and out at the city, where lights were coming on for the 4. ________, then glanced back down at the article. There was a paragraph she hadn't noticed before. "Specialised in criminal 5. ________, international business, immigration and – ." She couldn't read it, so she looked out over the city again. When she looked down once more, the words were more readable: "Specialised in criminal law, international business, immigration and immigrants' rights." "I suppose," Dr Black thought, "those could be rather depressing 6. ________, but international business is the place to make a lot of money." She looked back down at the

7. ____________________ and the article continued. Successful practice. Recent illness and depression. Overwork.

"The stress of the work affected him," Dr Black thought. "The pressure of making sure that innocent people didn't get sent to jail. There was also the pressure of making sure contracts between companies in different countries were legal as well as beneficial to the company he represented; the pressure of ensuring that the companies' practices were legal within the country where they had branch offices; the pressure of negotiating with the government to make their practices legal. Then there were immigration cases: keeping families together; keeping asylum-seekers safe. Such cases were not about money but people's families and lives. A strange mixture of specialities, however," she thought. "Normally a solicitor specialises in just one of those areas."

Übung 73: Beantworten Sie die Fragen zum Text!

1. Did Dr Black take a taxi to the office building?

____

2. How old is the newspaper Dr Black read in the penthouse office?

____

3. On what floor is the penthouse office located?

____

4. How did Dr Black get into the penthouse office?

____

5. How many people did Dr Black speak to on the eighth floor?

6. What does she read about in the newspaper?

Finally, it was too dark to read, but Dr Black remained seated at the desk. The office was absolutely quiet. Nothing moved if she did not move. Nothing made a sound if she did not trouble to make a sound herself. Every now and again, in the dark, she felt the hair stand up on the back of her neck. "It's only your imagination running wild," she told herself, "Think about something else, about somewhere else." She looked around in the dark to see if there was anything to see and found herself relieved that she could see nothing. The darkness was nearly complete, and was probably as complete as it would be for the night. "I wish I'd brought a candle; perhaps the next time I come here I will."

Übung 74: Lesen Sie weiter und unterstreichen Sie die Gegenteile der Wörter in Klammern!

(old, presence, slowly, enemies, distant, health, answer, admitted, warmth)

ÜBUNG 74 !

To help her focus on something else, Dr Black thought about a case on which she had assisted Dr Grimes. A young man of 27 had thrown himself down seven floors, or that was the report. The family, the father and mother especially, were certain it was murder, since there was no suicide note. Without any evidence of murder, and the lack of a suicide note, there was not enough to make the police suspect murder, there was no case, so the police handed the matter over to Dr Grimes. Dr Grimes had learnt rather quickly who was in the young man's circle of friends, had soon after found out who had access to the parents' flat and had discovered the nature of the family relationship. She soon convinced Dr Black that close observation of the father would uncover a family secret, which included not only a history of abuse but a history of illness, mental illness. On certain days, the father answered the same question in one way and on other days in another way. Dr Grimes and Dr Black concluded that the father had been the one who had thrown the son from the balcony. One day he denied it with a vehemence that was heartbreaking; another day it aroused fear in Dr Grimes, fear of the older man who had all the coldness and arrogance of a military officer.

Finally, the old military officer had admitted that he had told his son that he was not good enough. There had been a discussion and the father had told the son what he had to do: career steps he had to take. The son, who had always felt his father's judgement but who now knew for certain what his father thought, finally rebelled against him. The old officer was unprepared for this and threw him from the flat's balcony. He explained to the police what he had done, but later that day, in jail, he remembered nothing of his confession. Dr Grimes had, with much effort, convinced the police that his denial was real: he did not remember making his confession and he was sick. The case had been the only time Dr Black had come into contact with a suicide, and it had turned out to be a murder. The young man's friends had all been saddened by his death, for they had valued the quiet young man.
Dr Black got up from the desk and wandered through the office and the conference rooms. She looked out onto Manchester once again. It was a symphony of lights, a myriad of colours – red, yellow,

green, white, blue and various shades of these colours. She looked out at the city in all four directions of the compass; she looked for the red fog, imagining that, should it form, then this site would provide an excellent point from which to detect it. Though she never felt quite comfortable in the abandoned office, she didn't even consider leaving it until nearly 10.45 pm.

"I must get home to Eugene," she thought. "There'll be nothing more to see tonight."

Übung 75: Welche Farbe beschreibt welches Substantiv? Ordnen Sie zu!

1. red	☐ sky
2. blue	☐ night
3. yellow	☐ blood
4. green	☐ snow
5. black	☐ sun
6. white	☐ grass

It was only as she was leaving the office that she suddenly felt extremely frightened. A chill raced up and down her body, making the hair on her arms stick up and giving her goose pimples. She pulled the office door closed and began to quickly descend the stairs. On the eighth floor, she ran to the next set of stairs, which would take her to the ground floor. Going down these stairs, she expected at any minute to come face to face with some sort of ghost or demon, if either apparition could be said to have a face. The darkened windows acted like a wall: she could scarcely see any lights from the city coming through them. "Run," she said to herself, "run." Down she went, to the ground floor, where she suddenly and for no reason expected to find the front doors chained shut. To her great relief, they were locked but not chained, and she ran out of the building and all the way to her scooter. She glanced back up at the building. The penthouse office, which she hadn't noticed before from the outside, seemed to be sleeping quietly. Dr Black, however, felt quite agitated herself, so that she shook as she started her scooter and pulled out into the street.

Übung 76: Setzen Sie die richtigen Präpositionen in die Lücken ein!

(of, into, out of, from, of, up to)

Dr Black ignored Weatherly as she walked 1. __________ the back door 2. __________ her house. While unlocking the door, she could hear moans 3. __________ Eugene. He raced 4. __________ the house and down the four steps. Then he ran straight 5. __________ the middle 6. __________ the small yard and relieved himself against the wall.

"Oh you poor little creature," she said to him in the baby voice that only he inspired. "Mummy's so sorry she left you inside so long." She went in the kitchen and got him some dinner, then she opened a bottle of red wine for herself and sat on the back steps, facing Weatherly's little house.

The night had cooled down considerably, but Dr Black did not notice the cold. Eugene sniffed around in the backyard, enjoying his freedom for the first time in hours. Weatherly came outside and saw Dr Black sitting on the steps.

Übung 77: Übersetzen Sie!

1. schmecken ______________________
2. tasten ______________________
3. zuhören ______________________
4. riechen ______________________
5. berühren ______________________
6. hören ______________________

"Fancy a glass of wine?" she offered. "It's a dry French red of the kind that Dr Grimes used to have on hand."
"That would be lovely, if it's not too much trouble," he answered, walking up to her.
Dr Black returned with a second glass and the bottle of wine, and they sat quietly, both watching Eugene who continued to explore the grass. He went slowly from spot to spot, inspecting the earth as if a regular army of animals had crossed the almost enclosed backyard during the day. Dr Black took a sip of wine and then began to tremble. Her shoulders and knees began to shake.

Übung 78: Unterstreichen Sie die richtige Alternative!

"I reckon you're getting (1.) hot/cold," Weatherly observed.
"No, it's not that," she (2.) answered/asked and then described her trip to the office building, telling Weatherly everything she had seen.
"I'm not sure I understand," Weatherly admitted when she had (3.) begun/finished. "You have this picture of a man pop into your head,

you think he's the one in the (4.) newspaper/magazine – but I don't see how that relates to this red fog."

"I don't either, Weatherly. Not really. The (5.) next/other night when we followed the red fog, it brought us to that building, and I thought that there might be some reason. If there (6.) are/is, I still haven't found it."

"The red fog that only you could see."

"Are you trying to say you don't think it's real?"

"Not at all."

"Good. (7.) Tomorrow/Yesterday afternoon, we're going to go up to the penthouse office again, with candles this (8.) mall/time, and we're going to see if anything happens."

"What are you expecting to (9.) happen/pass?"

"Nothing, (10.) really/real. Perhaps we'll see the red fog, perhaps not."

"Perhaps *you'll* see the red fog."

The following day, Dr Black had several appointments in the morning, so the middle of the afternoon came around quickly. She drove her scooter to the office building and waited for Weatherly, who had taken the bus, to appear.

"This isn't efficient at all," Weatherly had complained upon leaving. "I really do think you're going to have to seriously consider buying a car one of these days. There's no Tube, as there is in London, and even the Tube isn't always convenient."

Sometime close to five o'clock Weatherly arrived and was in no better a mood than he had been upon his departure. He followed Dr Black into the building and up to the fifth floor in the lift. From there, they took the stairs up to the eighth. Wandering around the eighth floor, they looked at the city and Dr Black pointed out the sights to Weatherly.

Übung 79: Steigern Sie die Adjektive!

1. good ____________ ____________
2. fast ____________ ____________
3. bad ____________ ____________
4. quick ____________ ____________
5. few ____________ ____________

"This city doesn't inspire me," he grumbled, "the way London does."
"You have to open yourself to Manchester," Dr Black said. "And you have to be a bit more active. Manchester is a very lively city. If you want to enjoy it, you have to go to it. You can't just be an observer here."
"There's nothing to observe in Manchester unless you can look down on it like we're doing," he said.
"You'll think differently if you stay here long enough. It grows on you."
"Like a fungus."

They left the windows and walked to the stairway that led to the penthouse office. Weatherly went first, glancing up the stairs towards the door.
"You broke the door," he said.
"I told you that already. I had to."
Weatherly mounted the stairs slowly, and Dr Black followed closely behind him. At the top of the stairs, he pushed the door open and walked into the office Dr Black had left the previous evening.

"You needn't be so cautious, Weatherly. I was here last night. It's safe. This is the outer office."

"I am always cautious, Dr Black," he said quietly. "I never assume any place is safe. It is my business to be cautious. I am responsible for making sure that no one, myself included, is hurt. If someone or something comes around the corner, I want to be prepared."

"Nothing's going to come around the corner."

"You *expect* nothing to come around the corner, which doesn't mean that nothing *will* come around the corner."

ÜBUNG 80 !

Übung 80: Übersetzen Sie und enträtseln Sie das Lösungswort!

1. immer _ _ _ _ ☐ _
2. sicher _ _ _ ☐
3. jemand ☐ _ _ _ _ _ _
4. verletzen _ _ _ ☐
5. bedeuten _ ☐ _ _
6. Ecke _ _ ☐ _ _ _
7. hinter _ _ _ _ _ ☐
8. Tag _ ☐ _
9. gelb ☐ _ _ _ _ _

Lösung: _ _ _ _ _ _ _ _ _

Weatherly entered the two conference rooms, and searched the solicitor's office. He explored each room in the office thoroughly, opening all drawers, tapping on the walls and moving pictures. On finishing, he returned to the newspaper on the secretary's desk. "This is the person who popped into your head? John William Johnson?"

"That would be the one."
"Who names a child John Johnson? William Williamson? James Jameson? I knew a boy named Michael K. Michael. Mick Michael, he was called."
"It does seem tactless."
"It says here that he threw himself from the eighth floor. The secretary must have read it on her last day at work and left it here. I can't blame her for not wanting to take it home." Weatherly read the article and then placed the candles on the desk and walked away from it.

Übung 81: Übersetzen Sie die in Klammern stehenden Wörter!

They wandered about a bit more, and then they (1. beide) ________ sat down, Dr Black on a chair that had once held clients filling in (2. Fragebogen) ________ for the secretary and Weatherly on a sofa. Neither was really sure what they should do while they were waiting. Weatherly furthermore had no idea what they were waiting for and for that (3. Grund) ________ was rather impatient.

"So, we just sit here?" he asked her. "And we're not really waiting for anything? We're just sitting in an abandoned office to see if (4. etwas) ________ or anything happens?"

"It sounds stupid, I know, but I just have a (5. Gefühl) ________ that something is going to happen or that something is happening."

"That something *is* happening? What?"

“I don’t know.”

At this confession from Dr Black, Weatherly stood (6. wieder) __________ and began to walk around the room. He walked into the office, and then into each of the conference rooms, and finally (7. zurück) __________ over to the secretary’s desk. He leaned over her desk and began to (8. lesen) ________________ the article on the solicitor who had killed himself.

“I don’t remember reading that (9. vorher) _________,” Weatherly said after reading silently for a moment.

“What don’t you remember?”
“It says here that Johnson left a note behind.”
“I don’t remember that either,” Dr Black said, getting up. “In fact, I thought it said that no note had been found.”
“We both must have overlooked it,” Weatherly said.
Dr Black read the article again and there, towards the middle, it said that the police reported finding a note.
“I read this last night,” she said, “and I don’t remember that being in there at all. In fact, I remember thinking that there was no mention of a note. Somehow this article seems different. Most of the facts are the same, but it somehow seems different.”
Dr Black walked over to the windows that looked out onto the Arndale and studied the city. The sun was setting slowly on what had been a rather grey spring day. “It’s the beginning of April,” she thought. “We should be seeing buds soon and, hopefully, in a few months, everything will be blooming. I’m so sick of grey, and Manchester is beautiful in the summer.”

This last thought she repeated loudly to Weatherly.
"If you say so, Dr Black. I reckon I'll find out for myself."
Dr Black walked back over to the newspaper and, leaning over it once again, read the article. She stopped in the middle of it, and almost let out a scream. Weatherly noticed something in her expression and the way she was reading. She was scowling. Her fist suddenly went up to her mouth, and she began biting her knuckles.

Übung 82: Vervollständigen Sie die Sätze mit ***a, an, the*** *oder* ***that****!*

"There's something in 1. _____ article that wasn't there before," she said at last. "When we read this article half 2. _____ hour ago, it said that Johnson left a suicide note. Now, Weatherly, it reports on the contents of 3. _____ note. He said that he was disgusted with himself for having helped too many criminals go unpunished. 4. _____ sentence was not there. I thought I'd read the article to 5. _____ end yesterday as well, and then you mentioned that the police had found 6. _____ note. I thought I'd simply been hasty or careless. Maybe I'd been nervous and simply not seen the last paragraph."
Weatherly read over her shoulder. "7. _____ wasn't there before. I would stake my life on it. I read the article from beginning to end, and that was not there."

"If it wasn't there, then what is it doing there now?"
"That I can't answer, Dr Black, but I can tell you that the descrip-

tion of the suicide letter was not there. I'm sure about it."
"We have to look a little closer at this newspaper, Weatherly. I don't think we've seen anything like this before."
"Never seen a paper before?"
"Not one that writes the news."
"I wonder if any of the other stories have changed."
They read a couple of other stories on the front page, one about the then Prime Minister John Winston and another about a proposed tax increase.
"Now we walk away from the paper and wait a bit," suggested Dr Black. "And, no, I don't know how long."

ÜBUNG 83 !

Übung 83: Lesen Sie weiter und unterstreichen Sie die richtige Alternative!

Weatherly first (1.) light/lit the candles that he had put on the secretary's desk, and then he stepped away. They (2.) wondered/wandered nervously, now, around the large office. They (3.) stopped/stepped into the solicitor's own office, making wide circles around the secretary's desk, trying not to get (4.) to/too close for fear that their presence might somehow prevent the newspaper (5.) from/for doing whatever it would naturally (6.) did/do.
"Or our presence might prevent the newspaper from doing (7.) was/what it might unnaturally do or what it might supernaturally do," thought Dr Black a little playfully.
"It's now eight o'clock," Weatherly (8.) says/said. "I wonder if we should expect anything else."
"In addition to waiting to see what develops with the newspaper, I'd like to at least stay (9.) until/under ten o'clock because each time I've seen the red fog it's been somewhere around that time."

"I expect that the excitement caused by the newspaper will (10.) made/make our time a little more interesting."

Weatherly walked over to the newspaper and began to read it again. First he read the article about the solicitor, then he read the one about John Winston and finally he read the article about the tax increase. Nothing was obviously different: there was no new information that he was sure hadn't been there in the previous reading, and there didn't seem to be any other changes.
"I don't see any changes yet," he reported. The candles, quite near him, flickered a moment. "What was that?" he asked. "There's no breeze in here."
"I didn't see anything," Dr Black said.
"I'm probably a bit nervous."

Übung 84: Beantworten Sie die Fragen zum Text!

ÜBUNG 84 !

1. In what manner does Weatherly enter the penthouse office?

2. What form of lighting do Weatherly and Dr Black bring with them to the penthouse office?

3. What is so special about the newspaper on the secretary's desk?

4. What is the most recent piece of new information in the article on John William Johnson?

5. Who decides they will stay until 10 pm?

____

6. Why does he/she choose that time?

____

____

They waited and waited in the darkness lit only by three candles. They wandered from room to room; they sat and chatted quietly, discussing experiences. Several times they returned to the newspaper, but nothing more happened. They looked out the windows to see if a red fog had formed over any part of the city, but they observed nothing. At 11 pm they finally left the penthouse office.

Übung 85: Ordnen Sie die Buchstaben zu einem sinnvollen Wort!

"We'll come (1. kbca) __________ tomorrow about the same time," Dr Black said, putting the candle out.

In the (2. sskadrne) ______________, they were both a bit disoriented at first. Both wanted to get out of the building as quickly as (3. ssbileop) _______________. Their own movements made them a bit uncertain and each hoped the other was making the sounds that suddenly seemed to be coming from everywhere.

"Wait," Dr Black called.

Neither of them (4. devom) ______________. They stood still and waited, listening.

"What are we waiting for?"

"I heard so many (5. dnosus) ____________ suddenly that I thought maybe I was hearing more than us."

"When you lose one of your senses," Weatherly explained, "the (6. retohs) ________ become sharper."

"That may be, but I don't like that explanation."

"You'd prefer to think that there was a (7. driht) ______ person in here with us?"

"I prefer," said Dr Black, "to be able to rely on my (8. eesssn) _______ to provide me with the correct information. But I think it really was nothing, just nerves, blood rushing to my head."

Once outside they were both able to relax a little.
"That started out interesting enough," Weatherly said, "but it seems like it was a waste of time in general."
"I don't understand that at all. I wouldn't call it a waste of time. The newspaper shows that we are definitely on the right track. I plan on being here again tomorrow night, with or without you."
"Naturally I'll be right at your side. I'm just not sure I agree with the necessity of staying here for hours. I'll be very interested to see if there have been any changes to the newspaper articles tomorrow."
Weatherly sat on the back of Dr Black's scooter and the two of them made their way home rather slowly. They stayed off the major roads and drove instead through residential areas.
"That would be fun," Weatherly said, as he got off the scooter, "if it could go a bit faster. I would also prefer a helmet, but I reckon my head is hard enough to withstand a fall at such low speeds."

Übung 86: Welches Wort ist das „schwarze Schaf"?

1. rush, hasten, hurry, stroll
2. house, home, flat, hallway
3. fun, look, games, play
4. darkness, night, dawn, stars
5. enjoy, smell, touch, taste
6. newspaper, magazine, documentary, book

The next morning, while Eugene was walking in the backyard, Dr Black sat in the doorway to her yard, drinking a cup of tea. The sky was blue and the day promised to be warm. She could hear the sound of hammering, of a hammer hitting a piece of metal, in the servant's house. Eugene too heard the sound and was distracted from what he was doing.

"What are you doing, Weatherly?" she asked at the doorway to his house.

"I'm still fixing the sink. If I hadn't been sitting around with you yesterday evening, I'd have been finished with it by now. As it is, I have been a bit delayed with my repairs."

"You still think it was a waste of time," Dr Black said. "I don't understand that."

"It's just that this morning it seems a bit unreal. Normally, for me, it's the exact opposite. Things seem even more real in the morning."

"Today I suspect we may see how real things are."

Übung 87: Setzen Sie die Verben in Klammern ins Simple Past!

As Dr Black and Weatherly (1. be) __________ entering the building later that day, they (2. run) __________ into a middle-aged woman who, because of her light-blue uniform, they (3. think) ________ was someone who (4. work) ________ in housekeeping. Dr Black (5. ask) ________ her about the top three floors, intentionally not mentioning the ninth floor.

"I don't go up there. No one goes up there anymore. I (6. not be) ________ here when it (7. happen) ________, but ever since that solicitor (8. jump) ________ to his death, no one goes up there anymore. Within two months of his death, all the firms on floors six, seven and eight had moved away. I've only heard what others have said, but since I don't have to go up there I don't."

"But what do they say?"

"I'm not saying I believe it myself, but they say that something's not right up there, that there's something up there and it's neither man nor beast. That's all they say, and I don't pretend to know anything more than that."

"Does anyone clean those floors?"

"I don't think so. I don't think anyone goes up there. It's been closed for years. The lift doesn't even go up there anymore."

"The owner's content to leave three floors of his office building empty?"

The woman from housekeeping shrugged her shoulders. "The people from the eighth floor left quickly. Those from the seventh and sixth floors left a month or two later. Everyone expected the offices on the fifth floor to be empty soon as well, but it didn't happen that way."

"All the same, that's three floors."

"I should think," Weatherly said, jumping in, "that he's glad to be able to rent out the rest of it."

ÜBUNG 88 !

Übung 88: Welche Gegenteile gehören zusammen?

1. empty	☐ reject
2. quiet	☐ accidental
3. glad	☐ rise
4. fall	☐ full
5. intentional	☐ loud
6. choose	☐ unhappy

Dr Black and Weatherly took the lift to the fifth floor. On the way up, they discussed what might have led the other firms to choose to leave their offices. "Perhaps the other firms had law practices similar to that of John Johnson," Dr Black suggested.

"You think they were haunted, then?" Weatherly asked.

"That I can't say for sure," replied Dr Black "but they might at least have had guilty consciences."

"A solicitor with a conscience: that's a rarity." Weatherly laughed, but it was not a friendly laugh.

"A conscience," Weatherly added, "is an absolute handicap for a solicitor. Most of those villains have absolutely none. If they had one, they'd knock it around on a billiards table rather than be guided by it in consultations with clients or whilst standing in front of a judge. A conscience would be a terrible failing in a solicitor. You can't lie, withhold information and deny what you know to be the truth if you have a conscience."

"Okay, Weatherly, I get your point." Dr Black hadn't yet got used to Weatherly's extreme points of view.

"And your fees cannot be extremely high either."

"I haven't seen your fees yet, Weatherly."

Übung 89: Gibt der Satz den richtigen Sachverhalt wieder? Markieren Sie mit richtig ✔ oder falsch – !

ÜBUNG 89 !

1. Weatherly respects solicitors. ☐
2. The building was not cleaned after Johnson's suicide. ☐
3. Weatherly doesn't want to stay in the solicitor's office longer than necessary. ☐
4. Dr Black is waiting for something but still does not know what it is. ☐
5. Dr Black and Weatherly have forgotten all about the newspaper. ☐
6. Weatherly and Dr Black have the same opinion about everything. ☐
7. The solicitors and their staff on all the floors left the building after Johnson jumped to his death. ☐

They walked up through the sixth, seventh and eighth floors, looking in all directions. Dr Black felt as if she had not properly considered things before. These floors and the ninth floor were, perhaps, not as harmless as she thought. They took the stairs up to the ninth floor, Weatherly again leading the way, and looked into the gloomy office. Though the day was quite nice outside and the sun was still relatively high in the sky, here it was dark. They immediately walked over to the newspaper and began to read the article on the solicitor.

"It's different," Dr Black said almost immediately.

"The story keeps rewriting itself," Weatherly said.

"Now there's a quote from the suicide note."
"I've never seen one published in a newspaper before, especially not a respectable one."
"Maybe," she agreed, "but it is here in this one: 'All I ever wanted was to be a good solicitor, and I've become a good one – but I'm a good solicitor in a bad cause and that I cannot live with. I wish I could make the criminals pay for their activities, but I'm helpless to change the system. If my death shakes up this old and corrupt profession, then I will have done something good.'"
"There's a solicitor I should like to have met," said Weatherly.
"Maybe you'll get a chance," Dr Black said, a wicked smile on her face. "The article on the tax increase is shorter, and there's a small article I don't remember seeing before. Charles Gibson. He's the man who was found bound and gagged. His wife and her lover were responsible, but after they made it to the train station it wasn't clear where they went next. It says here that the two went to Italy, to Florence, where they stayed in a flat. He has disappeared again, but she has been found absolutely insane. Sunburnt and hearing voices. The woman had no prior record, but the man had a criminal record. It doesn't say what he did."
"How can an article on a crime that was committed only a couple of weeks ago suddenly appear in a newspaper that was printed six years ago?"

Übung 90: Setzen Sie die richtigen Präpositionen ein!

Dr Black looked (1.) _____ the date at the top (2.) _____ the newspaper, which was still the same, and then looked at the date at the beginning (3.) _____ the article.

"It's dated tomorrow," Dr Black said, amazed. "The article is dated tomorrow."

Weatherly looked at the article and then walked away (4.) _______ a moment.

"Perhaps," she suggested, "the newspaper is reporting the future somehow. It may very well be that (5.) _____ the moment the couple (6.) _____ the article are sitting quite happily in one of Florence's beautiful piazzas. They're sitting and thinking that they've somehow managed to escape the police as well as the woman's husband. They've committed the perfect crime and are free to spend the rest (7.) _____ their lives (8.) _____ unmarried happiness."

Weatherly returned and looked through the article himself. "It says here that this Mr Gibson has apparently decided not to file charges, or that he hasn't filed any charges yet, in any case. You don't suppose the old boy has gone mad himself? He loves his wife so much that he's going to just let her go or, worse still, he's going to wait for her to come back?"

"I'm just wondering about the significance of this date. Tomorrow. How can that be? We have a lot to learn about this newspaper."

"Yes," Weatherly answered. "For instance: who is it for?"

"Does this newspaper just sit up here and make its little changes for the pure joy of it? Impossible. It would just be a magician's toy, admittedly an extraordinary one. The changes about the solicitor are interesting, but they don't really matter. This article about tomorrow, though, that's information for someone or else it's revealing the future."

"Someone must read it and then act upon what's written there."
"Or someone's actions are recorded here before they take place. We're going to find out whose."

! ÜBUNG 91

Übung 91: Welche Zeitausdrücke gehören zusammen?

1. 5 am	☐ noon
2. 8 am	☐ the witching hour
3. midday	☐ dawn
4. 1 pm	☐ dusk
5. 11 am	☐ dinner time
6. 8 pm	☐ breakfast time
7. 10 pm	☐ lunch time
8. midnight	☐ mid-morning

The sun set slowly over Manchester, and Weatherly once again lit three candles on the secretary's desk. They walked around a bit, but unlike the previous night they sat much of the time in silence. It was as if by common agreement that they knew that someone or something was coming, and this was a certainty that they had not known the previous night.
It was some time after nine o'clock when they noticed a pink glow beginning to seep into the room. It started at the ceiling and spread around the room. Neither Dr Black nor Weatherly spoke a word after Dr Black whispered, "Look." Weatherly nodded his head as if to say, "Yes, I can see it this time." They simply watched the progress of the change. Pink turned to red and eventually to blood-red. It was a glow rather than a fog, although like a fog, something seemed to be floating in the coloured area: it just wasn't clear what was floating.

Übung 92: Wie lauten die Wendungen? Ordnen Sie zu!

1. to shrug	☐ one's head
2. to point	☐ one's nose
3. to shake	☐ the thumbs up
4. to throw up	☐ one's finger
5. to nod	☐ one's shoulders
6. to blow	☐ one's hands
7. to give	☐ one's head

"From the outside," Dr Black thought, "people must be able to see this red glow: it's impossible that this should only be on the inside." The room was flooded. Only the candles provided light of another colour, a yellow which, when mixed with the red, became orange, but only in the immediate area of the candles.
Then, into the room walked a very real John William Johnson, straight from his own office. Wearing a blue-white pinstriped suit, he looked rather thin but otherwise no different from his photo and no worse for his fall from the eighth storey. Apparently there was much to do. The candles on the desk went out as he sat down at the secretary's desk and immediately began to read the newspaper in front of him. He read for several minutes in complete silence, unaware of the two people in his outer office. In the air around him the glow seemed to be a bit thicker, more fog-like but not as thick as the fogs Dr Black had seen on the streets of Manchester or in the skies overhead.

Übung 93: Bringen Sie die Wörter in die richtige Reihenfolge!

1. contain of lots newspapers information daily

---

2. rather John William Johnson thin looked

3. brightly the candles the desk burned on

4. finds interesting he that

5. desk candles out the went the on

6. newspaper read the today they

"Anything interesting?" Dr Black asked at last, her voice clearly revealing her nervousness.

John William Johnson looked up immediately, his eyes went from Dr Black to Weatherly and back to Dr Black, and then he returned to reading the paper.

"We don't seem to be a threat to him," Dr Black thought. Then she added, "He must see the article on himself. Does he find that interesting? Or is he reading the article on Gibson?"

"There's an interesting article on a solicitor," she said, her voice still weak, "in the middle of the front page, towards the bottom."

"Indeed?" he asked, without raising his eyes from the newspaper. "And why is an article on a solicitor of any interest? There's so much more of importance in a newspaper: what's on television tonight; which Hollywood actors are falling in love, which are getting married and which are getting divorced; which models are trying a new diet and how good this diet is for you. You, too," he said, looking at Dr Black, "can lose five stone in a week. There's so much important information in the newspaper."

Übung 94: Fügen Sie die Übersetzung der in Klammern stehenden Wörter ein!

"Sarcasm," thought Dr Black. "This is one (1. verärgerter) ________ man or solicitor or whatever he is."

"Perhaps," Weatherly joined in, "there are (2. andere) ________ articles of interest on the front page."

"Which would you (3. vorschlagen) ____________________?" he asked, looking up. "The article on that mediocre (4. Politiker) ________________ John Winston? A nice man, John Winston, but he needs a little spice in his life. Mary Barnstorm (5. zeigte) ____________ him how it was done, but it turns out he doesn't have enough (6. Eisen) __________ in his blood."

"Actually," Dr Black suggested, "there's an article on a Mrs Dolores Gibson and a Mr David Knight that might be very interesting."

"I thought so as well," John William Johnson answered. "Quite a story. Yes, this David Knight and this Dolores Gibson – they really (7. spielten) _________ a nice trick on her husband, didn't they? They tied him up and left him to die. To starve, more accurately."

"A rather painful death," said Weatherly, involving himself in the conversation.
"Rather," answered John William Johnson. "A gruesome death if you have nothing to drink. It isn't mentioned in the article, but he was actually tied up to a radiator, so he couldn't move out of the room. He couldn't just roll down the stairs and get something to cut his bonds. They tied him up so that he couldn't even get to the other side of the room. And what does the guy do? He refuses to file charges. She'd have seen him dead, but he hasn't the courage to see her in jail. I think, however, that she cannot go unpunished. Certainly this David Knight would have abandoned her once he saw his opportunity, but she doesn't see that yet. And some solicitor will likely find some way to protect her, to give her the benefit of the doubt, as they say. I would say, instead, that doubt is one thing we have little of. There is no doubt, for instance, that she wanted her husband dead: it was her idea to tie him to the radiator using a rope around his waist where his belt should have gone."

"And you have something to say to her about her actions?" Dr Black asked.
"I do indeed. In fact, she's already hearing from me. For several days now, she's been hearing screams and calls of people who were wronged but never saw justice. She doesn't hear the voices all the time, and she doesn't hear them only when she sleeps. She just hears them – occasionally. She wakes up and there's a red fog in her room. She walks into an art gallery, and Florence is filled with art galleries, and suddenly she's alone, and there's a red fog."
"You're playing with her."
"God forbid! Punishing her," whispered John William Johnson. "There is a difference, and it's all the difference in the world, don't you agree?"

Übung 95: Setzen Sie den richtigen Begriff in die Lücke!
(mediocre, punishment, interesting, daring, headlines, starve, diet, husband)

1. When you want to learn more about a subject, that subject is ____________________.

2. To die because you cannot eat anything is to ______________.

3. Someone who is average at something is ________________.

4. To eat carefully in order to lose weight means to be on a ______________.

5. To put someone in jail is a form of ____________________.

6. When a man is married, he is a ____________________.

7. At the top of the newspaper you find the ________________.

8. Someone who takes risks is ______________.

He got up and looked closely at the two of them and then walked into his office. Dr Black immediately stood and ran over to his office. Before she got to the door, she could already see that the room was filled with a red fog, a fog thicker than that in the waiting area, but she could also see that the office was empty. “Where did he go? There is nothing in here but furniture and fog.” She walked over to the window overlooking the city but could see nothing more than lights from neighbouring buildings and her own reflection. She thought: “You want to see something else, you want to learn about something else and you are forced to look at yourself once again, always forced back upon yourself.”

Walking back out of the solicitor's office, Dr Black came face to face with Weatherly.

"Is he gone?" Weatherly asked.

"Yes," she answered and then looked at him in the light of the candle he had lit. "You are now a very bright red yourself, Weatherly. It suits you," she smiled. "It makes you look years younger."

"I think we'd better leave immediately," he suggested. "If this fog, or glow or whatever it was, has attracted any attention, especially on the part of the police, I think it would be wise of us to leave here as quickly as possible. We don't belong here after all."

"They can search us, and they'll find out we haven't stolen anything."

"Do you really want to explain to them why we were up here at this time of night? Do you really want to explain this sunburn? We've just opened a new spa, for instance?"

"Weatherly, you do have a sense of humour! You should use it more often!"

ÜBUNG 96 !

Übung 96: Welche Wörter passen zusammen?

1. lose	☐ page
2. newspaper	☐ machine
3. front	☐ weather
4. answering	☐ weight
5. stormy	☐ suit
6. pinstripe	☐ in love
7. fall	☐ article

"That was an experience," Dr Black said, walking towards her scooter, "though I'm not sure what to make of it."

"You were just face to face with the dead."
"He didn't look very dead. I wasn't sure if we were ever in danger. Could you tell?"
"One is usually only in danger when the dead see you as a threat."
"Gibson and her lover were never a threat."
"He has other business with them. He wants to punish them."
"Because he thinks they will not be punished – and as a solicitor, in the past, he ensured that many people weren't punished. He's making up for his past mistakes."
"You must also consider, Dr Black, that someone who throws himself off a building feels very strongly about something, even if only for a little while, perhaps just the time it takes to get to the top of a building and make that leap into the unknown, into nothingness. Mr Johnson felt very strongly about something and quite clearly still does. He is not likely to stop caring from one day to the next."
"Which is another way of saying that John William Johnson is, indeed, a danger."
"In short, yes."

Übung 97: Unterstreichen Sie die passenden Wörter!

1. John William Johnson is a nice/an angry fellow.
2. Dolores Gibson is/is not a loving wife.
3. John William Johnson heard/read the newspaper.
4. Mrs Gibson and Mr Knight went to France/Italy.
5. The red fog was inside/outside the office.
6. Weatherly saw/did not see that John William Johnson was a danger.
7. Mrs Gibson and Mr Knight are safe/in danger.
8. Weatherly wants to stay in/leave the building after Mr Johnson leaves.

Dr Black dreamt of fires burning through forests, of animals running from their territory, of creatures unable to move quickly and burning in the fire's path. "Somehow," she thought, "I have to learn to control fire." Her dreams were vivid but did not disturb her sleep, so she woke in the morning rested. It almost made her feel uneasy when she thought how calmly she was able to handle, as Weatherly said, being "face to face with the dead." Weatherly, as could be heard clearly from Dr Black's kitchen, was at work in his house. He seemed equally calm about the previous evening's events.

ÜBUNG 98 !

Übung 98: Fügen Sie das Gegenteil der in Klammern stehenden Wörter ein!

That afternoon, Dr Black again took Weatherly on the (1. front) __________ of her scooter.

"Why are we (2. moving) __________ here?" Weatherly asked, as she stopped in front of a row of shops.

"I'll be (3. in) __________ in a minute."

She went into an off-licence on Oxford Road and in a couple of minutes (4. left) __________.

"Do you think it's (5. foolish) __________ taking alcohol with us tonight?" Weatherly asked, though he couldn't see any bottles. "It must be a (6. big) __________ bottle," he thought.

"I can't think of any other way to deal with it," she (7. asked) __________, and then got back (8. off) __________ the scooter and pointed it (9. away from) ____________ the city centre, the law building and the ninth floor office.

"We're lucky that security is relaxed around here," Weatherly said, as they went up the stairs from the fifth to the sixth floor.
"Security can't do much about such entities as John William Johnson," Dr Black said. "Otherwise, three floors and a penthouse office would not be vacant in the middle of Manchester."
Weatherly once again led the way up the stairway to the penthouse office. He gave Dr Black such a serious look that she followed him without a word. Once in the office, he moved quickly from room to room, surveying everything to make sure no one and nothing was there. Convinced that they were alone and in relative safety, Dr Black followed Weatherly to the secretary's desk and to the newspaper on it. They both leaned over it to look for new articles and any changes in the ones they had read the previous evening. The article on the solicitor was different but not in any important way. Now there were witnesses, and someone had attempted to talk him out of jumping.

Übung 99: Ordnen Sie die Buchstaben zu einem sinnvollen Wort!

! ÜBUNG 99

"The (1. etarilc) ____________ on Mrs Gibson and Mr Knight is now longer," Dr Black said, scanning the article. "The (2. etda) ____________ on the article is now tomorrow – which should come as no surprise, I suppose. But she's been (3. dnouf) ____________ dead."

"There were blisters all over her face and arms, but the cause of her (4. thead) __________ is not reported."

"We'll likely have to (5. twia) __________ until later tonight or tomorrow or some other time to find out (6. tjus) __________ how she died."

"And I reckon we'll find out about Mr Knight then, as well."

"Weatherly, we do have to (7. khtni) __________ about how to stop this John William Johnson," Dr Black said, walking away from the (8. aryretsec) ____________________'s desk. She looked out onto a rainy Manchester. "The rain cannot (9. nleca) __________ this city any more than one dead solicitor can," she said to herself. "One person cannot clean a (10. ycti) __________ and certainly not in the way that he is going about it."

Before stepping away from the wet window, Dr Black saw her reflection. There was her face, a young face still, with dark hair down to her shoulders. On her face she saw a few small blisters. "Do these blisters," she wondered, "mean that I am in the same boat as Dolores Gibson?" She walked out to Weatherly.
"I have blisters as well," she told him.
"I noticed. I'm also sunburnt. It is only a matter of time until blisters appear on my face and hands."
"But we aren't his targets. We have broken no laws. We haven't escaped from anything. We haven't escaped from anybody's justice."
"Except his."

"I can't believe that this sunburn means our end as well. If he were to kill us, he would be acting as unjustly as those he condemns. He would be a hypocrite." She walked around the large waiting room. "You don't really think that would bother him, do you?"
"We don't know the cause of death, do we?" Dr Black asked, thinking aloud and ignoring Weatherly. "It hasn't shown up in the newspaper yet. It's not worth wondering about at the moment."
Weatherly lit three candles and sat down on the couch. "There have been plagues in the past, when people's faces blistered. That is, you and I might describe their faces as blistered, perhaps, but doctors would probably use other words. The fact is, we don't have any other symptoms yet."
"So let's not worry. Or, we'll worry when we have other reasons to worry."
"We'll worry if he gives us a reason to worry."
"I suppose he's given us plenty to worry about, but not in respect of our own safety."

Übung 100: Fügen Sie die richtigen Präpositionen ein!

1. Dr Black takes long walks with Eugene ______ the weekend.
2. John William Johnson has been dead ______ six years, according to the newspaper.
3. Weatherly lived ______ London before moving ______ Manchester.
4. Manchester is a lovely city ______ a holiday.
5. Nigel and Richard live ______ a dark side street.
6. The penthouse office is ______ the top of a tall building.

"Look at this other article," Dr Black said. "Look, this article on a possible tax increase. Now there's another report right below it. On Nigel Jones-Smith. Unemployed, petty thief, with a criminal record. Robbed a tea service valued at £11,000 which was later recovered by the owner at a pawnshop. I helped Mrs Nelson retrieve that tea service, Weatherly."

"We should be looking at this newspaper much more carefully. So far, we have only really looked at the front page. But we must go through it page by page and look at the dates of the articles."

They searched through the newspaper, and on each page they found more people mentioned. The farther back they went, the farther back in time were the dates on the articles. Most of the deaths appeared to be accidental deaths. Many people simply walked in front of cars. Others fell from high buildings but were not suspected of having committed suicide. Some drowned in pools or in lakes while sailing. Several died in house fires. Each person, however, came from Greater Manchester and came to an end, a definite end. And in each newspaper article some crime or other, usually theft but occasionally murder, was reported. It was always a case, though, that had puzzled the police, and there was never a report that the police had succeeded in solving anything.

"One man is a police officer, judge, jury and executioner," said Weatherly.

"And a solicitor."

Dr Black turned the newspaper back to the front page and, looking at the picture of the solicitor, said, "This isn't fair. You have no right to do what you have done. You are just a killer. You are worse than the people you punish. You stink worse than they do. Most of them never killed anyone and never would have killed anyone if they had been allowed to live out their lives. The killers among your victims have not killed as many people as you have."

“I expect that will make you feel better,” Weatherly said to Dr Black, “but I can’t say that I think it will have any effect.”
“I wouldn’t be so sure, Weatherly. There’s more to this newspaper than meets the eye. You’re going to have to believe me on that.”
“I don’t need convincing. What exactly do you believe it is?”
“A portal.”

Übung 101: Übersetzen Sie die Wörter in Klammern!

It was several minutes after Dr Black had last checked her (1. Armbanduhr) ______________, which had then showed 9.13 pm, that the (2. rosa) ______________ glow began to once again slowly fill the room. It worked its way in at the (3. Ecken) ______________ and edges of the office and slowly changed to red as it filled the room, as if stretching out thousands of arms and legs one by one. They watched a slow (4. Flut) ______________ of pink and red enter the room from (5. oben) ______________ and work its way down to the floorboards and the floor.
Dr Black looked at Weatherly, who (6. nickte) ______________ to acknowledge that, once again, he saw the colour. It was suddenly something of a (7. Geheimnis) ______________ to her why he had been unable to see it on the night in the car but was now, here in the penthouse office, able to see the fog. “Did the fog simply not show itself to him then, or is there something about this location

that is different?" she asked herself. "That really doesn't matter, I suppose. I'd better focus on things that do matter. For instance, did I (8. rief) __________ John William Johnson or was he going to come here anyway? If I summoned him, he may behave differently than he did last night. He may not be so (9. tolerant) __________."

The room now seemed to be bathed in a blood-red, foggy glow. There was something in the glow, still, which made it a fog, although not a thick fog. "Maybe what we're seeing is him," thought Dr Black. "The red fog is his blood and whatever it is that is moving in the fog is somehow him or the "him" that we will see soon. Yesterday the fog was thickest in his office just after he left. Does the fog serve him? Or does he serve the fog? Or is he the fog?"
"Do you think he's coming, Dr Black? Yesterday he was here far sooner. The red fog or glow has been here now for quite some time."
"I don't know. We're going to stay here as long as the red fog does. That's all I know for sure."

ÜBUNG 102 !

Übung 102: Unterstreichen Sie die richtige Form des Verbs!

And so they (1.) waiting/waited. But it (2.) was/were not a comfortable period. At any moment, they expected (3.) seeing/to see the solicitor step through the door of his office into the waiting room, and they (4.) were/was again and again disappointed. Refusing to stay seated any longer, Dr. Black walked over to the desk and (5.) looking/looked again at the front page of the newspaper. She looked for the article on Dolores Gibson and David Knight and then read through it quickly, looking for new information. The report (6.) begun/began this time with news of Mrs Gibson's death but now included something new about Mr Knight: David Knight had been hit by a car and killed in Sicily at sunset. The driver of the car, who (7.) working/worked for the Mafia and was suspected of participation in a number of "disappearances", had gone through the windscreen and had joined Mr Knight in death. Dr Black (8.) was scanning/scanned the rest of the article but came across nothing new.

"Even as we sit here," she said to Weatherly, "someone is dying or has died. This article carries today's date."
"Check the one on Nigel Jones-Smith," Weatherly suggested.
She found the article quickly and again scanned through it.
"Whereabouts unknown," she read aloud to Weatherly.
"That sounds dangerous. And the article on John William Johnson? Read through it quickly."
"I am." She went through the article as quickly as she could. "He had been under investigation for – it doesn't say. Perhaps doing whatever it took to get his clients free."

Übung 103: Welche Wörter gehören zusammen?

! ÜBUNG 103

1. quick	☐	risky
2. unknown	☐	figures
3. dangerous	☐	mysterious
4. numbers	☐	decease
5. comfortable	☐	fast
6. death	☐	responsible
7. trustworthy	☐	relaxing

"Come over here, Dr Black," Weatherly said. "It's clear as day."

She immediately left the area of the desk but stood only a short distance from it. The fire at the tips of the candles died and she ran up to the desk and quickly retrieved them. At that moment, in walked the same young lawyer, dressed and looking just as they had seen him the night before. And just like the previous night, he sat down at the secretary's desk and began reading the paper, again without even pausing to greet his uninvited guests.

Dr Black and Weatherly watched John William Johnson closely. "Are we invisible until we speak," she wondered, "or does he just enjoy being the centre of attention? He will only speak to us when he feels he is ready. He either wants to make us wait, or he wants to force us to take the first step. Well, I don't mind taking the first step."

"Anything new in the newspaper?" she asked with unmistakeable irony.

Not even taking the time to look up, John William Johnson lifted a pale index finger and tapped it lightly on the newspaper twice and all but the smallest of his fingers slowly followed one two three, one two three, one two three. Then he lifted his head up and tilted it to the side as if, finally, he was curious about their presence.

"You're back," he said matter-of-factly.

"You're back," Dr Black answered in the same tone.

"You are funny," he returned.

"Reports of your death seem to be greatly exaggerated."

"On the contrary, nothing could be closer to the truth."

"So, you are dead?"

"Don't you recognise sarcasm when you hear it?"

"What are you doing here?"

"You've been reading the newspaper, haven't you? There's really no need for me to explain further, is there?"

Übung 104: Bilden Sie die Verneinung der Sätze!

1. Dr Black has got a big American car.

2. Weatherly is trying to make John William Johnson go to Liverpool.

3. The building looks like one of the Houses of Parliament in London.

4. They will be very hungry late in the day.

John William Johnson went back to reading the newspaper, as if his daughter had disturbed his reading and had, finally, gone to some other part of the house to play, leaving him to enjoy his peace.
Weatherly quietly came up to Dr Black and lit her candle. “Be diplomatic,” he whispered. “Remember, we could be in real danger.”
“I’ll try,” she answered.
“I have read the newspaper,” Dr Black said, once again addressing John William Johnson. “You are quite right. I have noticed that many people have died in rather mysterious circumstances, though it’s only in that newspaper, accompanied by so many other similar

stories, that they appear mysterious. The one thing that seems to unite all these people, besides their mysterious deaths, is that they were guilty of some crime. None of them, however, appears to have even been considered by the police as a suspect."

"Certainly some people have been helped to their deaths, their small, unimportant deaths. There has been, of late, an attempt to aid the police. So far, however, you are the only one who has been able to see the red fog. People cannot be made to see what they will not see. The best that can be done, however, is to make sure that when people are being robbed they remain asleep so that they are in no danger. The perpetrators of the latest crimes have been marked with sunburn and yet the police force remains blind."

"I have been marked, too," said Dr Black. "I have sunburn even though I committed no crime."

"You stood in the fogs and heard the singing of the sirens," he smiled. It was the mean smile of an executioner. "You listened to them."

"You have no right to be a judge and an executioner. What I read in the newspaper of a young solicitor concerned about the lack of fairness in the world is not answered by the list of deaths that fill the pages of that newspaper."

"The world isn't fair; it isn't a fair place at all. The weight has to fall somewhere, the weight of right and wrong, so why should there be any consideration of fairness? Cutting off the hand that steals, as they did in England and elsewhere in the world hundreds of years ago, didn't stop stealing. It made stealing a necessity because a man who survived losing his hand could no longer do most jobs. Even if there has been no fairness, then at least the world is now a better place."

"The world is a better place without Nigel Jones-Smith? Except for burgling the tea service, what has he really done?"

"He has stolen cars and gone for what the Americans vulgarly call

"joyrides". He has stolen other items, all of lesser value, it is true, but there's a pattern."
"And now he's missing? We might presume him dead, I suppose?"
"Oh, he's not dead, not just yet. But let's just say that time is not on his side. Youths usually feel that they have all the time in the world, and poor Nigel the petty thief no longer does."

Übung 105: Markieren Sie folgende Aussagen mit richtig ✔ oder falsch – !

1. There is no connection between the fog and the burglaries. ☐
2. Dr Black doesn't care what John William Johnson does. ☐
3. There is not much security in the building with the penthouse office. ☐
4. Weatherly thinks he and Dr Black are quite safe. ☐
5. John William Johnson is wearing a business suit. ☐
6. When the fog is in the office, the room is very dark. ☐
7. Mrs Gibson and Mr Knight are mentioned in the newspaper. ☐

Dr Black looked at John William Johnson, who stood and rested his fingertips on the top of the desk.
"I really can't believe," she said, "that you feel that what you are doing is justified."
"I do nothing. I am doing nothing."
"You're not responsible?"
"No. They are."
"Who is this "they"? The voices I heard in the fog? The people who were screaming? They're responsible?"

"They're the conscience that every solicitor who defends a guilty person should hear."

John William Johnson turned towards his office and began to walk away. Weatherly ran up to Dr Black.

"Now is the time to do something, if you wish to save this Nigel."

Dr Black gave Weatherly her candle and then pulled out a can of lighter fuel and poured it onto the newspaper. Weatherly, who had moved to her elbow, dropped the candle on the newspaper.

Whoosh!!

A giant flame leapt up. Dr Black poured out more fuel, and a flame the size of a man reached towards the ceiling and scorched it. In the midst of the flame was a figure, distorted by colour and heat and pain. The newspaper even appeared to roll around in agony, though it never moved from its place on the desk.

"Again," screamed Weatherly.

She did as Weatherly said, and the great flame seemed to reach burning arms towards the ceiling.

Dr Black handed the lighter fuel to Weatherly and said, "Keep putting lighter fuel on it till there's nothing left of the newspaper." She then ran over to the office that John William Johnson had just entered. As she expected, there was no sign of him, nothing but smoke and fog hung about in the air. She returned to the waiting room where Weatherly was still looking at the fire.

Though the flames had now died down to a normal fire, burning a bit brightly for an ordinary newspaper and burning only on top of the desk, Weatherly added more fuel to the fire until there was nothing left to burn, until the pile of ashes sitting on the desk no longer bore any resemblance to a newspaper at all.

"It's over," Dr Black said.

"The red fog? I don't know."

"That was John William Johnson in the fire, I'm certain of it."

Übung 106: Welches Wort ist das „schwarze Schaf“?

1. chair, desk, table, toilet
2. ordinary, typical, usual, abnormal
3. cloud, moon, clone, sun
4. judge, barman, solicitor, defendant
5. carpet, mop, rug, tile
6. floor, ceiling, desk, wall

They left to explore what had once been the solicitor's office, but there was no sign at all of the fog that had followed Johnson the previous day. Dr Black looked down at the wall-to-wall carpeting on the floor of the office and saw three footprints lightly burned into it.
"How do you explain that?" Dr Black asked, kneeling to look a little closer at the footprints. They hadn't burned the carpet black; it was more as if it had been toasted. The synthetic material had, however, melted.
"How do I explain that?" Weatherly asked. "I don't."
"That wasn't a proper answer, Weatherly."
She glanced out from the office window onto the top of the building and saw no one and nothing. They walked back to the outer office area, and Weatherly stepped up to the desk. He reached his hand into the ashes, which were already getting cold.
"These are not the ashes from a newspaper," he said, "these are human ashes."
Weatherly pulled a letter opener from a drawer and poked through the ashes. The fine powder had cooled off quickly. He pulled a drawer out from the desk and swept the pile of ashes into it.
"What are you going to do?" Dr Black asked.
"I'm going to scatter these ashes to the four winds. If Mr Johnson wanted to protect Manchester that much, then perhaps he deserves

to be given a final resting place in the city streets he wanted to clean up."

They walked over to a glass door that led onto a small balcony, the last door that the live John William Johnson had passed through. With a gentle toss of his hand, Weatherly gave the wind all the ashes in the drawer and the two of them watched the ashes float quietly away.

"It reminds me of the red fog the night we followed it to this building in the car," Dr Black said, "except for the colour, of course."

"Now it's grey."

"I wonder if Nigel will turn up – alive."

"I can't believe that he just let us burn the newspaper," Weatherly said. "He never really attempted self-defence."

"Last night and tonight he put the candles out, but I believe he still had a strong sense of right and wrong. It's just that his sense of wrong was out of balance. He punished every crime the same way."

"Well, maybe now the building's owners will be able to rent out the rooms on the top four floors. I would suggest, once again, that we make a hasty exit, in case someone has noticed something suspicious."

They walked out of the building and over to where Dr. Black had left her scooter.

"Oh no," she said, and ran up to her scooter. It was now a smouldering ruin.

"What do you think happened?" Weatherly asked.

"I guess if you play with fire, you will get burnt," Dr Black said quietly.

"I think we'll have to seek an alternative form of transportation home tonight," Weatherly said, "and give this – ," he gestured with one hand towards what was left of the scooter, " – a proper burial tomorrow."

"Or," she continued thoughtfully, "does this mean he hasn't really gone?"

Abschlusstest

Übung 1: Welches Wort ist das „schwarze Schaf“?

1. fire, smoke, flame, brew
2. fog, mist, sun, haze
3. solve, explain, expert, unravel
4. strange, unusual, average, bizarre
5. hinder, help, assist, aid
6. leave, exercise, exit, depart

Übung 2: Fügen Sie die richtige Präposition ein!
(into, between, on, towards, by, in, for, from, to, of)

1. The ghost of John William Johnson came suddenly __________ the room.
2. Weatherly quickly lit the candles __________ the desk.
3. The shops were side __________ side.
4. Dr Black had been living in Manchester __________ nearly a year.
5. The newspaper was not __________ this world.
6. She handed the lighter fuel __________ Weatherly.
7. Weatherly took a match __________ his pocket.
8. The desk was __________ the centre of the room.
9. She moved slowly __________ the solicitor’s office.
10. They returned to the building __________ 6 and 7 o’clock.

Übung 3: Schreiben Sie die Sätze in der aktiven Form!

1. The car was driven by Weatherly back to Manchester.

2. Weatherly was sent to Dr Black by Dr Grimes.

3. The food dish was cleaned out by the dog.

4. The scooter was swallowed by flames.

5. Weatherly and Dr Black were seen as troublesome by the police.

Übung 4: Fügen Sie das richtige Fragewort ein!

1. ________________ old is Eugene?
2. ________________ time is it?
3. ________________ car is parked in front of my house?
4. ________________ did they have to leave so soon?
5. ________________ are we leaving for the party?

Übung 5: Welcher Satz enthält die richtige Übersetzung? Kreuzen Sie an!

1. Sie wohnt seit drei Jahren in Manchester.
   a) ☐ She lives in Manchester for three years.
   b) ☐ She has been living in Manchester for three years.

2. Er läuft gerade ins Zimmer hinein.
   a) ☐ He is walking into the room.
   b) ☐ He walks into the room.

3. Weatherly geht ihr auf die Nerven.
   a) ☐ Weatherly gets on her nerves.
   b) ☐ Weatherly goes on her nerves.

4. Sie mussten bis 10:30 Uhr wieder zu Hause sein.
   a) ☐ They had to be home until 10.30 am.
   b) ☐ They had to be home by 10.30 am.

5. Sie hat das Buch von der Bibliothek ausgeliehen.
   a) ☐ She lent the book from the library.
   b) ☐ She borrowed the book from the library.

Übung 6: Unterstreichen Sie die richtige Alternative!

1. She departed/arrived at a street of terraced houses over which the red fog seemed about to settle.
2. Except of/for the fog, which seemed to contain its own light, the street was now dark.
3. “Its/It’s almost midnight,” she thought, as she entered the house.

4. John William Johnson was certainly no friend of there's/theirs.
5. Weatherly remembered/reminded her that spirits can be dangerous.
6. She wondered/wandered around the empty offices.
7. The glow of/off the candles turned orange in the fog.

Übung 7: Bilden Sie aus dem Substantiv ein Adjektiv!

1. fright ....
2. hurry ....
3. curiosity ....
4. danger ....
5. cleverness ....
6. fog ....
7. suspicion ....
8. courage ....
9. reality ....
10. supernatural ....

Übung 8: Unterstreichen Sie die Gegenteile der Wörter in Klammern!
(safe, strange, evening, somebody, slowly, opened, forget)

"The city sent some men down this morning, and they repaired all of them. I wondered about that. It's the first time I remember the city fixing anything here so quickly. The lamps not working, that I heard about, but I don't know anything about a red fog."

"Well, the lamps should be working tonight. Did you happen to speak to any of your neighbours today? Did any of your neighbours notice anything last night around 10 pm or so?"

"Nobody mentioned anything. Around ten you say? I probably closed the curtains around then, because I fell asleep early. I slept quite well, I did. My little girl slept until six o'clock this morning which was nice, but I didn't notice anything out of the ordinary. Is this red fog dangerous then?"

Übung 9: Übersetzen Sie die in Klammern stehenden Wörter!

"What don't you (1. erinnern) ______________?"

"It says here that Johnson left a note behind."

"I don't remember that either," Dr Black said, getting up. "In fact, I (2. dachte) ______________ it said that no note had been found." She walked over to the desk to look again at the newspaper.

"We both must have overlooked it," Weatherly (3. sagte) ______________.

Dr Black read the article and there, towards the middle, it said that the police reported finding a note.

"I read this (4. gestern Abend) ______________," she said, "and I don't remember that being in there at all. In fact, I remember thinking that there was no mention of a note. (5. irgendwie)

__________ this article seems different. Most of the facts are the same, but it somehow seems (6. anders) __________." Dr Black walked over to the windows that looked out onto the Arndale and studied the city. The sun was setting (7. langsam) __________ on what had been a rather grey spring day. "It's the (8. Anfang) __________ of April," she thought. "We should be seeing buds soon and, hopefully, in a few months, everything will be blooming. I'm so sick of grey, and Manchester is (9. wunderschön) __________ in the summer." This last thought she (10. wiederholte) __________ to Weatherly.

Übung 10: Beantworten Sie die Fragen zum Text!

1. Was Dr Black the only one who could see the fog?

____

____

2. Did the police want Dr Black and Weatherly to help them?

____

____

3. How was Dolores Gibson driven mad?

____

4. Did John William Johnson die at the end of the story?

____

Lösungen

Übung 1: 1. warmth 2. sleep 3. brightness 4. cold 5. interest 6. beauty

Übung 2: 1. straight/winding 2. loud/quiet 3. whisper/shout 4. round/square 5. distant/close 6. safe/dangerous

Übung 3: 1. woke 2. busy 3. restfulness 4. clients 5. prepare 6. advertisement 7. bottom 8. mind-reader

Übung 4: 1. Urteil 2. glühen 3. starren 4. verbreiten 5. Gegenerklärung

Übung 5: 1. Dr Black had a weakness for her dog Eugene. 2. She got Eugene when he was a puppy. 3. Eugene's thoughts were very complex. 4. Eugene often got scared on walks and sat down on the pavement. 5. Eugene had to share his owner with strange occurrences.

Übung 6: 1. Dr Black had studied at the University of Manchester. 2. She finished her studies in psychology at the University of London. 3. Dr Black was always very passionate about what she did. 4. Dr Black had decided to return to Manchester.

Übung 7: 1. It was blood-red. 2. She found her advertisement. 3. She had been back for a month. 4. She studied at the University between the ages of 19 and 22. 5. She was Dr Black's mentor at the University of London. 6. She was born in Swindon.

Übung 8: 1. helmet 2. fog 3. scooter 4. determine 5. heaviness 6. lesson 7. clouds Lösung: loonies (Spinner)

Übung 9: 1. arrived 2. scream 3. about 4. from 5. of 6. out 7. for 8. its

Übung 10: 1. silence 2. stillness 3. except 4. passenger 5. briefcase 6. completely

Übung 11: 1. speak 2. previous 3. stroll 4. ordinary 5. certain 6. several 7. sense 8. seemed

Übung 12: 1. b 2. a 3. b

Übung 13: 1. ordinary 2. reach 3. school 4. interest 5. handsome 6. right

Übung 14: 2. 12 Uhr 3. 24 Uhr 4. 6:30 Uhr 5. 22:30 Uhr 6. 2:45 Uhr

Übung 15: 1. repeated 2. wearing 3. darkness 4. strange 5. thought 6. coincidence 7. hide 8. drugs 9. unusual

Übung 16: 1. He was reading The Sun. 2. No, he didn't see the fog. 3. He took them to Piccadilly Station. 4. They were wearing sunglasses at night. 5. No, only Dr Black saw it.

Übung 17: 1. ticket counter 2. railway station 3. streetlights 4. taxi driver 5. first class 6. police officer

Übung 18: 1. She was a wild and crazy woman. 2. She reached for her sunglasses and put them on. 3. She stood there in her bathing suit. 4. So she poured a glass of water over her head to calm herself down. 5. "What pretty paper!" she thought.

Übung 19: 1. She asked the stranger to come straight to the point. 2. She didn't trust appearances. 3. His hair was slowly thinning. 4. Dr Black hated to be distracted. 5. He pulled a newspaper from his briefcase.

Übung 20: 1. weitermachen 2. sich etwas ausdenken 3. festhalten an 4. herumführen 5. sich trennen von 6. sich kümmern um

Übung 21: 1. d 2. a 3. f 4. b 5. e 6. c

Übung 22: 1. building 2. distance 3. living room 4. occasionally 5. expected 6. usually 7. ruins 8. furnish 9. pieces of furniture 10. suitcase

Übung 23: 1. type 2. familiar 3. likelihood 4. away 5. experience 6. caught

Übung 24: 1. immediately 2. pavement 3. library 4. lowering 5. stretching 6. streetlamps 7. disappear

Übung 25: 1. began 2. saw 3. came 4. got 5. felt 6. went

Übung 26: 1. lower 2. scream 3. caution 4. attempt 5. dishes 6. pavement 7. tremble 8. library 9. yard Lösung: Weatherly

Übung 27: 1. bedroom 2. undressed 3. jumped 4. slipped 5. sheets 6. realised 7. explain 8. sunburn

Übung 28: 1. a 2. b 3. a

Übung 29: 1. up 2. into 3. for 4. on 5. in 6. inside

Übung 30: 1. explain/make clear 2. remember/recall 3. hurt/harm 4. seem/appear 5. drop by/visit 6. discover/find out

Übung 31: 1. He wanted to offer her his help. 2. Dr Grimes gave it to him. 3. Because she thought he might have something to do with it. 4. She heard screams from men, women and children. 5. Yes, she got sunburn. 6. Only Dr Black saw it. 7. She told her that a neighbour was found half-starved and tied up.

Übung 32: 1. watch closely/observe 2. plan to do something/intend 3. take something away/remove 4. have much to do/be busy 5. steal something/rob 6. permit/allow

Übung 33: 1. demand 2. nightclub 3. caring 4. catch 5. turn 6. cold

Übung 34: 1. employ 2. separate 3. explain 4. estimate 5. surprise 6. agree

Übung 35: 1. They drove away together. 2. She was back from her holiday. 3. Only Dr Black saw the red fog. 4. She went to bed early. 5. Weatherly was very tired.

Übung 36: 1. women 2. lost 3. died 4. hero 5. certain 6. remembered 7. suspects 8. crowd 9. ring

Übung 37: 1. Mrs Nelson's tea service was stolen. 2. The tea service was from Queen Victoria. 3. Mrs Nelson's son is a wild young man. 4. She wondered if the son had stolen the tea service 5. The fog always came while a crime was being committed.

Übung 38: 1. as 2. like 3. as … as 4. like 5. as … as 6. like 7. as 8. like

Übung 39: 1. c 2. b 3. c 4. b

Übung 40: 1. evidence/proof 2. hint/clue 3. criminal/thief 4. suspicious/questionable 5. solve/explain 6. detect/observe

Übung 41: 1. Richard's mother defended his reputation. 2. The neighbours gossiped about her son. 3. She knew the thief would have sunburn. 4. Dr Black did not get her sunburn at the beach. 5. She solved the mystery of the tea service.

Übung 42: 1. ghost 2. boy 3. starve 4. time 5. drop 6. cup 7. stranger Lösung: obvious

Übung 43: 1. polite/rude 2. understandable/confusing 3. quick/slow 4. late/early 5. show/hide 6. back/front

Übung 44: 1. weren't 2. got 3. answered 4. said 5. wasn't 6. took 7. gave 8. shouted

Übung 45: 1. bedroom 2. flatmate 3. pawnshop 4. peacekeeping 5. teaspoon 6. folk-song

Übung 46: 1. to 2. with 3. at 4. by 5. in

Übung 47: 1. Where 2. Who 3. What 4. How/Where 5. What/Which 6. Why

Übung 48: 1. pulled 2. noticed 3. moving 4. hit 5. turned 6. drove 7. get

Übung 49: 1. lorry 2. office 3. pedestrian 4. driver 5. entrance 6. speed

Übung 50: 1. Because it was given to her family by Queen Victoria. 2. He stole it to get money to live on. 3. She suspects Nigel may be the driver. 4. A crime is committed each time the fog appears. 5. She identified the person by his sunburnt skin.

Übung 51: 1. tee (tea) 2. bear (bare) 3. cheep (cheap) 4. pieple (people) 5. since (sense) 6. seam (seem) 7. werk (work)

Übung 52: 1. regret 2. clever 3. none 4. present 5. report

Übung 53: 1. The woman was almost run over by a lorry. 2. She did not trust new people right away. 3. She relied on her instincts to find the criminal. 4. She hoped to solve the mystery. 5. Weatherly did not care too much for the city of Manchester. 6. His experience was a valuable tool in solving the mystery.

Übung 54: 1. same 2. yours 3. save 4. night 5. drive 6. hour 7. story Lösung: mystery

Übung 55: 1. train 2. aeroplane 3. car 4. vehicle 5. underground 6. bicycle

Übung 56: 1. success/failure 2. someone/no one 3. natural/artificial 4. nothing/something 5. closing/opening 6. for/against

Übung 57: 1. The man was tied up by the woman and her lover. 2. The fog was only seen by Dr Black. 3. The fog was followed across Manchester by Weatherly and Dr Black. 4. A difficult decision was made by Dr Black. 5. Weatherly was sent to Dr Black by Dr Grimes.

Übung 58: 1. again 2. very 3. badly 4. just 5. however 6. outside

Übung 59: 1. scary 2. dangerous 3. injured 4. handsome 5. beautiful 6. brave

Übung 60: 1. It was dancing around to loud music. 2. British people like sun. 3. They wondered what on earth had happened to Winston Churchill. 4. The main meal is served around 6 pm.

Übung 61: 1. don't. 2. you're 3. Aren't you 4. we're 5. can't 6. It's

Übung 62: 1. office/building 2. time/clock 3. fog/weather 4. spring/season 5. police/order 6. fear/feeling

Übung 63: 1. problem 2. police 3. streets 4. night 5. business 6. sunburn 7. solicitor 8. criminals 9. thing 10. special

Übung 64: 1. distressed 2. was 3. thought 4. said 5. began

Übung 65: 1. b 2. c 3. c 4. a 5. b

Übung 66: 1. first 2. second 3. third 4. fourth 5. twentieth 6. twenty-second 7. ninety-ninth

Übung 67: 1. falsch 2. falsch 3. richtig 4. falsch 5. richtig 6. falsch 7. falsch

Übung 68: 1. armchair 2. desk 3. drawer 4. file 5. curtains 6. cabinet

Übung 69: 1. In 2. There's 3. ugly 4. beyond 5. somewhere 6. two 7. from 8. between

Übung 70: 1. foolish/stupid 2. knock/tap 3. attempt/try 4. almost/just about 5. steps/stairs 6. floor/storey

Übung 71: 1. She 2. He 3. him 4. We 5. They 6. them

Übung 72: 1. article 2. born 3. note 4. evening 5. law 6. subjects 7. newspaper

Übung 73: 1. No, she drove her scooter. 2. It is six years old. 3. It is located on the ninth floor. 4. She broke down the door. 5. She spoke to no one, except herself. 6. She reads about the solicitor's suicide.

Übung 74: 1. old/young 2. presence/lack 3. slowly/quickly 4. enemies/friends 5. distant/close 6. health/illness 7. answer/question 8. admitted/denied 9. warmth/coldness

Übung 75: 1. red/blood 2. blue/sky 3. yellow/sun 4. green/grass 5. black/night 6. white/snow

Übung 76: 1. up to 2. of 3. from 4. out of 5. into 6. of

Übung 77: 1. taste 2. feel 3. listen 4. smell 5. touch 6. hear

Übung 78: 1. cold 2. answered 3. finished 4. newspaper 5. other 6. is 7. Tomorrow 8. time 9. happen 10. really

Übung 79: 1. better, best 2. faster, fastest 3. worse, worst 4. quicker, quickest 5. fewer, fewest

Übung 80: 1. always 2. sure 3. someone 4. hurt 5. mean 6. corner 7. behind 8. day 9. yellow
Lösung: yesterday

Übung 81: 1. both 2. forms 3. reason 4. something 5. feeling 6. again 7. back 8. read 9. before

Übung 82: 1. the 2. an 3. the 4. That 5. the 6. a 7. That

Übung 83: 1. lit 2. wandered 3. stepped 4. too 5. from 6. do 7. what 8. said 9. until 10. make

Übung 84: 1. He enters cautiously. 2. They bring candles with them. 3. The articles change. 4. There is a description of the suicide note. 5. Dr Black decides they will stay until 10 pm. 6. She chooses that time because that is when she has usually seen the fog.

Übung 85: 1. back 2. darkness 3. possible 4. moved 5. sounds 6. others 7. third 8. senses

Übung 86: 1. stroll 2. hallway 3. look 4. dawn 5. enjoy 6. documentary

Übung 87: 1. were 2. ran 3. thought 4. worked 5. asked 6. wasn't 7. happened 8. jumped

Übung 88: 1. empty/full 2. quiet/loud 3. glad/unhappy 4. fall/rise 5. intentional/accidental 6. choose/reject

Übung 89: 1. falsch 2. falsch 3. richtig 4. richtig 5. falsch 6. falsch 7. falsch

Übung 90: 1. at 2. of 3. of 4. for 5. at 6. in 7. of 8. in

Übung 91: 1. 5 am/dawn 2. 8 am/breakfast time 3. midday/noon 4. 1 pm/lunch time 5. 11 am/mid-morning 6. 8 pm/dinner time 7. 10 pm/dusk 8. midnight/the witching hour

Übung 92: 1. to shrug one's shoulders 2. to point one's finger 3. to shake one's head 4. to throw up one's hands 5. to nod one's head 6. to blow one's nose 7. to give the thumbs up

Übung 93: 1. Daily newspapers contain lots of information. 2. John William Johnson looked rather thin. 3. The candles on the desk burned brightly. 4. He finds that interesting. 5. The candles on the desk went out. 6. They read the newspaper today.

Übung 94: 1. angry 2. other 3. suggest 4. politician 5. showed 6. iron 7. played

Übung 95: 1. interesting 2. starve 3. mediocre 4. diet 5. punishment 6. husband 7. headlines 8. daring

Übung 96: 1. lose weight 2. newspaper article 3. front page 4. answering machine 5. stormy weather 6. pinstripe suit 7. fall in love

Übung 97: 1. an angry 2. is not 3. read 4. Italy 5. inside 6. saw 7. in danger 8. leave

Übung 98: 1. back 2. stopping 3. out 4. returned 5. wise 6. small 7. answered 8. on 9. towards

Übung 99: 1. article 2. date 3. found 4. death 5. wait 6. just 7. think 8. secretary 9. clean 10. city

Übung 100: 1. at 2. for 3. in, to 4. for 5. on 6. at

Übung 101: 1. watch 2. pink 3. corners 4. flood 5. above 6. nodded 7. mystery 8. call 9. tolerant

Übung 102: 1. waited 2. was 3. to see 4. were 5. looked 6. began 7. worked 8. scanning

Übung 103: 1. quick/fast 2. unknown/mysterious 3. dangerous/risky 4. numbers/figures 5. comfortable/relaxing 6. death/decease 7. trustworthy/responsible

Übung 104: 1. Dr Black hasn't got a big American car. 2. Weatherly isn't trying to make John William Johnson go to Liverpool. 3. The building doesn't look like one of the Houses of Parliament in London. 4. They won't be very hungry late in the day.
Übung 105: 1. falsch 2. falsch 3. richtig 4. falsch 5. richtig 6. falsch 7. richtig
Übung 106: 1. toilet 2. abnormal 3. clone 4. barman 5. mop 6. desk

Lösungen Abschlusstest

Übung 1: 1. brew 2. sun 3. expert 4. average 5. hinder 6. exercise
Übung 2: 1. into 2. on 3. by 4. for 5. of 6. to 7. from 8. in 9. towards 10. between
Übung 3: 1. Weatherly drove the car back to Manchester. 2. Dr Grimes sent Weatherly to Dr Black. 3. The dog cleaned out the food dish. 4. Flames swallowed the scooter. 5. The police saw Weatherly and Dr Black as troublesome.
Übung 4: 1. How 2. What 3. Whose 4. Why 5. When
Übung 5: 1. b 2. a 3. a 4. b 5. b
Übung 6: 1. arrived 2. for 3. It's 4. theirs 5. reminded 6. wandered 7. of
Übung 7: 1. frightened 2. hurrying 3. curious 4. dangerous 5. clever 6. foggy 7. suspicious 8. courageous 9. real 10. supernatural
Übung 8: 1. safe/dangerous 2. strange/ordinary 3. evening/morning 4. somebody/nobody 5. slowly/quickly 6. opened/closed 7. forget/remember
Übung 9: 1. remember 2. thought 3. said 4. last night 5. Somehow 6. different 7. slowly 8. beginning 9. beautiful 10. repeated
Übung 10: 1. No, Weatherly saw the fog in the penthouse office. 2. No, the police did not want their help. 3. She heard voices in her head. 4. It is unclear whether he died or not.